TECHNIQUES AND EXERCISES

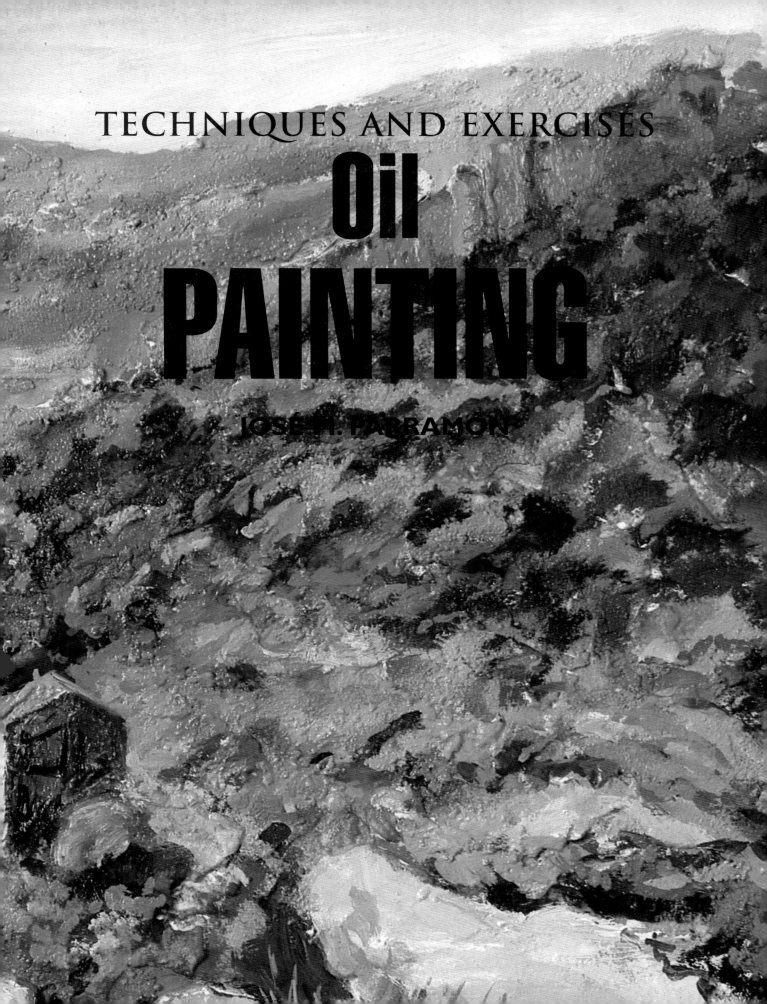

TECHNIQUES AND EXERCISES

Oil
PAINTING

JOSÉ M. PARRAMÓN

The guides at the end of the book are numbered in the margin and designed to be cut with a paper cutter.

Overall manager: José M. Parramón Vilasaló
Texts: José M. Parramón and Gabriel Martin
Editing, layout and design: Lema Publications, S.L.
Cover: Award and Lema Publications, S.L.
Editorial manager: José M. Parramón Homs
Editor: Eva Mª Durán
Coordination: Eduardo Hernández
Original title: *Pintando al óleo*
Translation: Mike Roberts

Photography and Photosetting: Novasis, S.A.L.

First edition: March 2000
© José M. Parramón Vilasaló
© Exclusive publishing rights: Lema Publications, S.L.
Published and distributed by Lema Publications, S.L.
Gran Via de les Corts Catalanes, 8-10, 1º 5ª A
08902 L'Hospitalet de Llobregat (Barcelona)

ISBN 84-95323-31-1
Printed in Spain

Index

Oils are one of the most widely used mediums, and throughout history they have been a favorite of the Grand Masters. This might be one of the reasons why so many people, when they take an interest in art for the first time, choose them as their first field of study. The use of mixtures of oils in domestic painting probably dates back to ancient times, although the term 'oil painting' is mostly used to refer to the procedures used in Europe towards the end of the Middle Ages. Since then, oils have come to symbolize the paintings of modern times. Over the space of a few decades, such techniques took the place of older methods, such as tempera, and brought with them a new support, canvas, which would eventually substitute the boards of prepared wood that had been used up until then. It appears that the oil painting technique was first introduced in Flanders at the beginning of the 15th century. Van Eyck is said to have been its inventor, although we understand that it was used almost simultaneously in some Italian workshops, in particular by Domenico Veneziano. We know of innumerable examples of the use of oils before the 15th century, but it was only later that it really became a new technique in itself. The new technique offered considerable advantages: better drying,

1

translucence up to transparency, the associated consistency and fluidity, delicate fusion of tones between two adjacent areas of color, and the possibility of new transparency effects from the background right up until the last layer on the surface. These possibilities reevaluated a type of work with depth whose results we find, many years later, in the works of Rembrandt, Rubens, Velázquez and Tiziano. These people took the technique to astonishing new heights, and it was thanks to oils that they achieved a subtlety and unlimited variety of effects in their paintings. Moreover, oil painting is the technique that presents the fewest differences between fresh and dry colors, making them the most appropriate for representations from nature in which everything depends upon the correct interpretation of tones. The adjustment of tones, along with the easy application and the fact that no other material can be used for so many modes of representation, mean that oil painting has practically superceded all of its rivals, although, at the turn of the millenium, acrylic paints are presenting strong competition. However, during the 19th century, groups appeared that were obsessed with the purity of the color that came fresh from the tube, something which the fauvists

could not resist, with their exaggerated expressiveness and little concern for adjusted tones, desperate to create optical vibrations on the painting surface and to build masses of color with thick pastes. It is only logical that oil painting has led the artist to discover truly enriched paintings by means of the material itself.

Although the novice artist might feel somewhat intimidated by the extensive history of oil painting and the elaborate techniques that have been used in some of the most famous works, oils are, in fact, an excellent medium for the beginner. Their flexibility and apparent ease of application, creating quick and immediate effects such as opacity and the characteristics of material, are among the reasons why oil painting has become the most widely used technique.

This book hopes to convince you of this and much more. From the very first pages, you will find useful pointers that will allow you first to understand the materials and later move on to practical study. You will also find illustrations of several pieces of work by professional artists along with exhaustive analysis.

Approaching the subject through a logical and practical method, I shall show you, step by step, how anybody

Fig. 1. **Belchite,** *by Teresa Trol (artist's private collection). Landscapes are the most popular oil painting subjects due to the quantity of different effects that this medium can produce.*

with sufficient interest in doing so can develop the necessary skills and techniques for oil painting. I hope that the guides that you will find at the end of the book, along with the texts and hundreds of illustrations that accompany them, are able to promote an uncontainable desire within you for painting with oils.

Gabriel Martín Roig
Art critic

Fig. 1. **Large nude** *(fragment), by Amadeo Modigliani (Museum of Modern Art, New York). Oil paints can be used for any type of treatment from meticulously detailed tonal paintings to large canvases covered with wide brushstrokes and plain colors, such as the example shown here.*

Fig. 2. Breton thatcher, *by Paul Sérusier (Haubergier collection, Senlis). The combination of the veiling technique and dry brushstrokes on a single support represent the light and atmosphere filtered by the dirty glass of the windows in this interior space.*
Fig. 3. Music party, Pertworth, *by William Turner (Tate Gallery, London). As the paint is denser than watercolors, it favors the effects created with a spatula, and the same goes for sgraffito and merging with the fingers.*

Fig. 1. The box of paints is a traditional element that can be used for storing and conserving paints, oil, varnish, tubes, brushes, spatulas, sponges and so on.

OILS:
MATERIALS
AND
EQUIPMENT

There is a wide range of oil painting materials
on the market, many of which are designed for
high quality use. Although a set of materials
can be expensive, if you are selective according
to your needs you can reduce the cost. If you
are a keen artist but still lack experience, the
texts and illustrations that follow should prove
extremely useful for getting to know
the materials and the wide range of basic
accessories that you are going to be working
with. These pages will also allow you
to compare and choose the right ranges of
colors, brushes, supports, solvents, mediums
and palettes that are best suited to your
individual needs.

Composition and Characteristics of Oil Paints

Oil paints are made of a pigment agglutinated with a natural drying oil, normally linseed, or a semi-drying one such as sunflower or opium. Its oily consistency tends to give the color richer shades, as well as making it a highly flexible medium that can be used in several ways, from a very thick paint to an extremely thin one (whose consistency is not far removed from that of watercolors).

Complementary resins and additive or drying products are frequently added to the paint, such as laminates and waxes that improve its flexibility and obtain a consistent texture and fast drying. The main advantage of oils with respect to other paints is their drying time; considerably longer than that of water or acrylic based paints. This makes them easier to manipulate and spread over the canvas to produce an endless variety of textures and effects. What does this imply? It implies that one can apply the paint to the canvas, scrape it, shape it, and even rework areas that were painted quite a while earlier, because the paint has not hardened yet. You will find that some colors take longer to dry than others. Earth colors act on the drying oils that agglutinate them, so they dry quite quickly, while others are much slower (some reds can take three or four days before they are dry to the touch).

Before starting to paint with oils, you need to think about one basic principle – that of always painting 'fat on lean'. This rule warns us that the painting should always be started by dissolving the paint with

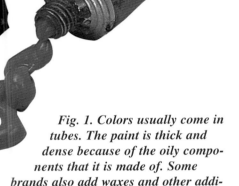

Fig. 1. Colors usually come in tubes. The paint is thick and dense because of the oily components that it is made of. Some brands also add waxes and other additives to get the right consistency.

Fig. 2. **Portrait of Claire Sennegon,** *by Camille Corot (Louvre Museum, Paris). If we study this portrait carefully we can see how long-lasting oil paints can be, but to take the right advantage of these properties, certain rules must be followed during the painting process.*

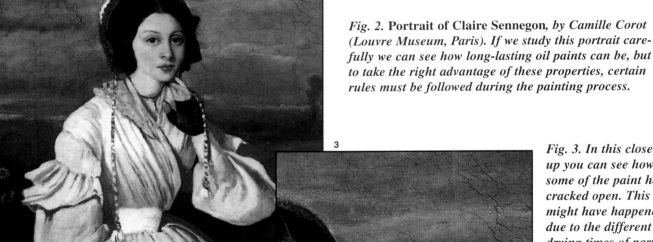

Fig. 3. In this close-up you can see how some of the paint has cracked open. This might have happened due to the different drying times of parts of the surface and the failure to observe the principle of 'fat on lean' and the adding of bitumen or wax to the top layer of paint.

turpentine essence (which is 'lean') and painting over it with linseed oil (which is 'fatty'). Alternatively, you can always paint with turpentine – first with the paint very diluted (lean) and then hardly diluted at all (fat). What you can never do is start with a fatty paint and finish off with a thinner one, because the paint would not stay on properly. As the paint dries, there is a good chance that the surface will crack up. Therefore, each layer must conserve its homogeneity and its proportion of liquid and avoid dulled tones by maintaining the pigment stable within the picture as a whole.

All decent brands of paint include a series of guidelines about their products. There is usually a series of details on the label of each tube but, in some cases, you need to consult the brand's color chart. It is important to study this information about the characteristics of the paints, even if only very briefly, before spending any money.

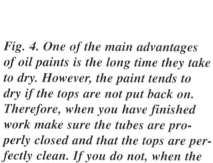

4

5

Fig. 4. One of the main advantages of oil paints is the long time they take to dry. However, the paint tends to dry if the tops are not put back on. Therefore, when you have finished work make sure the tubes are properly closed and that the tops are perfectly clean. If you do not, when the paint dries, the top will get stuck.

Fig. 5. You should start by getting a box and filling it with ten or twelve tubes of color, a selection of different brushes, a bottle of solvent, a palette... and then it's time to get working!

Range of Colors

Normally there are two types of oil paints available: colors for professionals and colors for amateurs. There is wider range of colors for professionals and the colors are more intense. Because of the origins of the pigments, these tubes are much more expensive. There is also a difference in the price of certain colors because some pigments are harder to get, which affects manufacturing costs, Others have a higher concentration of pigments, thinly agglutinated with higher quality oils, and are therefore more expensive too. The texture of professional colors tends to be softer, although this has no decisive effect on the appearance of the painting.

Colors for amateurs are elaborated with synthetic inks and cheap pigments that substitute cadmiums and cobalts, which are rarer and more expensive. Although they are equally permanent, their texture is much rougher because the pigments have not been ground so carefully. As they contain small qualities of fillings, such as chalk, the intensity of the colors may decrease slightly. There is also an enormous difference with respect to strength and brightness, particularly when they are mixed with white. Professional colors do not need so much to maintain the density of color. As both types can be mixed, they can be combined to keep down costs. Some professional artists use amateur colors to paint the base and use better quality paints for the outer layers.

Now that I have explained the basic differences between the two types of paint, I think I should point out that amateur colors are perfectly suitable for any beginning artist. When you feel confident enough you will be able to move on to colors of better quality.

Figs 1 and 2. With professional colors, you are guaranteed high quality pigments and agglutinates (fig. 1). Amateur paints, on the other hand, contain small quantities of chalk that, as well as acting as agglutinates, make the paint thicker (fig. 2).

Fig. 3. Instead of buying a box of professional paints, it is better to buy tubes individually. That way you will end up with the range of colors that best suits your needs.

Fig. 4. There is a wide difference in quality and price between paints for students and those for professionals. However, to keep down costs, they can both be combined in the same painting.

Oil Bars

For several years now, several manufacturers sell oil paints in the form of bars. They are a relatively new idea that has become popular with artists as they are so useful for making sketches.

At first glance, these sticks can easily be taken for oily or waxy pastel sticks. Their greater consistency owes itself to the combination of oil paints with special waxes that make the color more solid and consistent.

They provide several advantages, because they combine the richness of oil colors with the freedom and immediacy of pastels and charcoals. Their strokes are easily merged on the surface of the paper, either with the fingers or by diluting each stroke with a little thinners (one stroke of the brush or cotton wool soaked in turpentine is enough to blend the colors and obtain the same kind of pictorial effects as traditional oil paints). They also improve the fluidity of the color if the bar is simply dampened with thinners before applying it to the painting. A surface painted with oil bars is malleable enough to be worked with a spatula and to be corrected repeatedly. It is therefore important to take advantage of their innate characteristics and to combine them with traditional oils.

Once the lines drawn with the sticks are dry, it is impossible to erase or eliminate them because their consistency is very similar to that of a surface painted with oils. And although the drying time depends on the type surface to which the color is applied, they generally dry faster than traditional oils.

Unlike oils from tubes, it is not a good idea to mix different brands of oil bar because their chemical compositions are not always compatible.

Fig. 1. Oils are also sold in bar form, where the paint has been diluted with special waxes that give them a more solid texture.

Fig. 2. They produce similar strokes to waxes, but more broken, pasty, fluid and expressive.

Fig. 3. These bars can be diluted in turpentine essence to create washes that resemble those of traditional oils.

Fig. 4. As you can see, oil bars can not only be considered a painting medium, but a drawing one as well.

Agglutinates and Solvents

Oil paints contain three ingredients: the pigments (color particles), the agglutinate (the substance which permits the union of these and that fixes them to the support) and the solvent (the element that acts in a compound to get the right consistency). After studying colors in the previous chapters, we are now going to analyze the roles of agglutinates and solvents. Agglutinates are those simple constituents that come in liquid or creamy form and unite the pigment particles with each other, allowing the paint to be applied fluidly onto the surface of the painting. Oil is the agglutinate in oil paints, with gets harder as it dries and sticks the pigment onto the support, forming a compact mass. The agglutinate plays a specific role; brightness, transparency, dullness, absorption, pastes and cracking of the surface depend on it. Everything begins with the chosen oil, the way that it is treated, the mixtures that are included, its drying time and the degree of oxidation or yellowing.

For oil painting, only drying oils are relevant (which dry the oxygen out of air by absorption). Linseed oil, which is obtained from flaxseeds, is the most widely used. It dries very quickly at first, but the process can take years to finish. Opium oil is obtained by grinding the seeds of the opium plant, and it is used for slowing down the drying process of certain pigments. As it is more transparent and less prone to yellowing than linseed oil, it is often used for agglutinating white and light colors. Walnut oil is less solid and dries less efficiently than linseed oil. Other vegetable oils that are sometimes used are soya, sunflower and pine-seed oil.

Solvents are substances that lighten and reduce a mixture or dissolve the mass of paint. They are usually used to get a certain consistency of paint as one works, so that it thins or dilutes the paint and helps to spread it

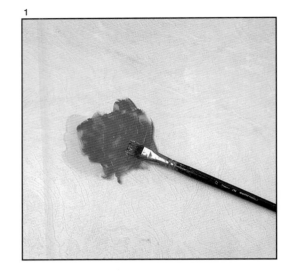

Fig. 1. The agglutinate of oil paints is oil. When it is mixed with the pigment, it creates a creamy paint, with intense colors and a characteristic shine.

Fig. 2. There is a wide range of oils: linseed oil, walnut oil, pine-seed oil, soya oil, sunflower oil, opium oil and others. Which you choose depends on your specific needs (drying time, degree of oxidization, yellowing, etc.).

over the surface of the painting in a fluid way. It can also be used for cleaning palettes and brushes. They are generally volatile liquids and turpentine is one of the most efficient. Turpentine essence (often called 'turps' for short) is a colorless product that is made by distilling conifer sap. This must always be rectified or distilled twice, because the type that is usually sold in hardware shops has a tendency to yellow the paint and make it sticky. Thinners are also used; a substitute for turpentine made from refined gas oil that evaporates quickly. It is becoming more popular as a solvent for several reasons. It is less damaging to the health, it does not spoil with age, it does not smell as strongly as turpentine and not only that, it's cheaper. Both can be used to dilute paint without any problems, but authentic turpentine is ideal for painting, while thinners is probably better for washing your brushes.

Simil is another solvent with the same evaporation qualities as thinners and turpentine. However, it does not smell so strong, does not spoil with age and is less flammable, making it less damaging to the health than the other two alternatives. Whether you are adding more agglutinate or more solvent to your paint, the operation should be carried out gradually and in small quantities. If you add too much agglutinate, in time the colors will yellow and darken more than necessary, while if you use too much solvent the resulting paint will form a layer of low consistency that could break up when it dries. Be careful.

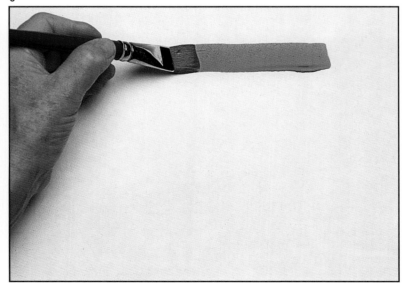

Fig. 3. Turpentine essence is obtained from the balm of conifers. With a transparent appearance and greasy feel, it is volatile, so the bottles should always be kept tightly shut.

Fig. 4. Thinners is a refined gas oil extract and is much more popular than turpentine. It used to produce a whitish film on the surface of a dry painting, but this problem has been overcome with improved formulas.

Fig. 5. Paint mixed with thinners or turpentine produces a very fluid stroke that can often resemble watercolors.

Mediums

Sometimes the oil paint that comes out of the tube is too dense, so the use of different drying oils, resins, varnishes and waxes, in combination with the paint, allows the artist to alter or highlight the characteristics of the colors.

Therefore, to get a more fluid color, solvents or mediums are used, which we discussed in the previous chapter. There is a wide range of mediums on the market. Some are mixtures of oil and varnish based on different traditional recipes; others are resins, produced by different manufacturers. Linseed oil has been the most popular medium throughout the centuries. Vasari suggested in the 16th century that oil "makes the color more morbid, sweeter and delicate and makes unions and merges easier than other forms, and as it is used, the colors mix together and unite with each other more easily".

Mediums, like solvents, can be used to thin out the paint, but also to improve its consistency and to increase the drying time.

However, there are other mediums that can alter the consistency of paint. For example, the medium for glazing that is often used in the veiling technique or the non-liquid medium that speeds up the drying process. Non-liquid resin is a translucent, synthetic material that is modified with oil and not only accelerates the drying time but forms a flexible film that does not yellow. Other drying agents include, for example, cobalt, which accelerates the drying of the oil, although its use is not advised for the veiling technique. It is more appropriate for pastes and surfaces painted with thick colors because it is not a very transparent product, and takes light out of veils and dulls their color. In such cases, it is better to use, for example, Dutch varnish, which might look dark and thick, but is transparent when it is applied. This varnish, used in measure for drying, when incorporated into the veil, gives it a shiny appearance that highlights the colors. Each brand markets its own particular drying agents. There are some mediums that can give a more enameled appearance to the paint, but more commonly does little more than darken it, so if you are going to use it you should bear this in mind.

Nearly all bottles have a label that explains the different attributes of the mediums in question. Remember that the ones that are prepared for painting are not standardized, so the formula of any given medium can vary from company to company.

Fig. 1. Dutch varnish is a medium that, despite its dark color, becomes transparent once it is mixed with the paint. This medium speeds up the drying of the paint.

Fig. 2. Mediums are additives that improve or alter the characteristics of oil paints. However, they should be used sparingly, because if they are applied excessively they can harm the agglutinate qualities of the linseed oil, which could cause the paint to crack when it dries.

Water-Soluble Paints

As some people are allergic to turpentine based products, or simply cannot stand the smell, some companies now market a paint that conserves all of the qualities of oils but that is soluble in water and has no smell. This means you do not have to inhale potentially dangerous vapors, which is particularly advisable if you are working near children. This paint has been created by chemically modifying the agglutinate (i.e. the linseed oil) so that it accepts water instead of repelling it. Water-soluble colors have the same characteristics as traditional oils (consistency, malleability and covering power) but dry much more quickly. Their colors are more lively and intense and their shine somewhat duller. At the moment, they are not available in as many colors as more traditional oils.

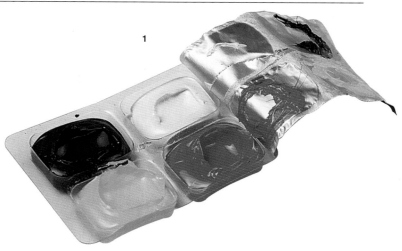

Fig. 1. These paints can be found in tubes and as capsules that can only be used once in all the basic colors and white. They are ideal for carrying in your pocket and for painting sketches outdoors.

Fig. 2. The range of water-soluble oils is not as wide as that of more traditional oils, but there are enough for you not to worry about the absence of any particular color. In any case, you can always mix the colors.

Fig. 3. If you go out into the country, it is a good idea to take a few small brushes with you, three or four capsules and a little notebook like this for making quick color sketches.

Basic Palette

It is important that the beginner artist makes his own selection of colors, based on evolution and personal needs. Remember that the color charts made by manufacturers include a wide range of different hues. Some color charts offer samples of more than 200 different colors (I once counted over fifteen different yellows in one). Of course, nobody uses that many colors.

It is important to start with a limited range of colors. Select a few fundamental colors, versatile enough to get a wide range of tones and shades by mixing them together. I would suggest the following as part of any basic palette: titanium white, yellow ochre, raw sienna, raw umber, burnt umber, carmine, cadmium red, cadmium yellow, cobalt blue, ultramarine blue, Prussian blue, permanent green and emerald green.

You can widen this range with one or more auxiliary colors such as Windsor violet, permanent red, cyan blue, ivory black or earth green, either because they are favorites of the artist or because the artist is going to paint a subject based around a particular color.

The most important color on the palette is white because it is used more than any other. Your whites should therefore be of extremely good quality. There are several on the market, but titanium white is probably the most versatile and reliable.

With the exception of white (which can be bought in a larger tube), tubes are available in two sizes. The 37 ml one is most practical for most colors. Amateur quality paints can also be purchased in 200-ml tins.

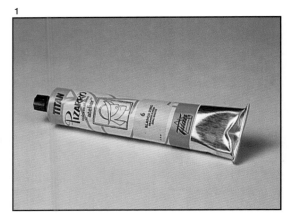

Fig. 1. In the adjacent figure, you have a chart of the colors that the artist uses most often. They are versatile enough for painting a wide range of subjects.

Fig. 2. White can always be purchased in a larger tube because it is the color that is used most often.

Preparing Colors on the Palette

The preparation of the palette depends on individual taste. However, to work fast and fluidly, and to be able to find the colors more easily, a strict order should be established and stuck to. Colors are usually ordered by temperature, being distributed from warm to cool (beginning with white, followed by yellow, orange, red, earth colors, and then black). They can also be arranged in the order of the spectrum or by separating warm colors from cool ones: red, orange and yellow on one side and green, blue and violet on the other.

The colors should be placed at the top of the palette with at least three fingers between each one. The paint should be squirted out as long strips so that color can be taken from both ends. By doing this, one end can be used for light colors and the other for darker ones. If you work in this way, the colors will stay cleaner for a longer time.

Fig. 1. The colors should be squirted onto the palette in long strips. This way colors can be taken from both ends, which means they won't get dirty so quickly.

Fig. 2. In the palette shown here, the colors are ordered from the warmest (on the right) to the coolest (on the left), with white as a divider. The other alternative involves arranging colors from the lightest to the darkest.

Mixtures of Oil Colors

This is an indispensable chapter in any book on oil painting – the study of mixtures of colors that determine the multitude of possibilities that exist.

According to the color wheel, all colors can be produced by mixing the three primaries, red, yellow and blue. Unfortunately, this is not really the case, because it is impossible to make some colors in this way (violets, purples, more intense greens and some blues).

Color purists prefer to apply color mixtures as complete pastes onto the canvas or support. Others mix them partially on the palette, and then finish creating the right shade on the canvas itself, mixing the two colors that were previously united. Mixtures can be made as pastes, streaks, sgraffito or pointillism, either on the palette or directly upon the support.

To paste mixtures of colors on the palette you do not need to use any diluting solution. This technique is intended for the times that colors are mixed on the actual support. A spatula is a very useful tool for mixing large quantities of paint and avoids wearing your brushes too much. However, if you want to work fast and just mix small quantities of color, brushes will suffice. When you use a brush to mix a color, you should use linear of circular strokes to minimize the amount of wear on your brushes.

Make sure that the mixture is uniform and there are no filaments of any other color. Take a test paper and apply the mixture to a white background to check that it looks right and that it really is the color that you are looking for. If it is not, rectify the color by adding new pigments and varying the proportions of the original mixture. Try to avoid using more than three colors in any one mixture. If you add more, the color loses intensity and looks too dark.

Fig. 1. Apart from fauvists, there are few people who paint with the color that comes directly out of the tube. You need to adjust the tones to match those of the subject and this involves mixing colors until you get the shade you are after.

Fig. 2. If you want to find out how two colors react to each other, make simple tests like these. Then try to add a third color to the resulting mixture (white, yellow, light blue) to find out how they react and what new ranges can be created.

Fig. 3. Colors should be mixed on the palette, although some artists like to mix them directly onto the support. You can use a conventional wooden palette or improvise one like this, which has been covered with a disposable sheet of plastic.

When you mix two colors and one color clearly dominates over the other, you should first apply the less
dominant color, and gradually add the dominant one
until the tone you wish to reproduce appears. This
way you can control the mixture better and use your
colors more economically by only making the color
that you are actually going to use.

After each mixture, make sure that you clean the
palette and any brushes you have used, or you could
spoil later mixtures with any leftover paint that is hidden within the bristles. At the end of each painting
session, clean everything before putting it away. We
will talk in detail about brush care in a later chapter.

4

*Fig. 4. When you mix large quantities
of paint on the palette, it is a good
idea to use a spatula rather than risk
wearing out your brushes.*

5

*Fig. 5. More than three colors should
never be included in a mixture. If we
follow this basic rule, our work can
look as crystal clear as this Brook
by Óscar Sanchís (artist's private
collection).*

*Figs. 6 and 7. Practice mixing colors
on a separate piece of paper to see
how different pigments react to each
other and what colors can be created.
First, use primary colors and then
move on to using secondary ones.*

6   7

Effects with the Brush

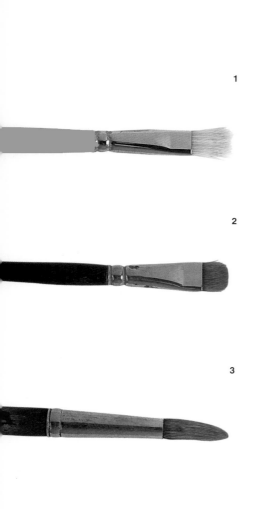

A painter can choose from the several different types and qualities of brushes that are available in all kinds of shapes and sizes. Better quality brushes may cost more, but are worth the investment. They hold the paint much better, last longer, hold their shape for more time and also retain it much better after they are washed. The most interesting ones are studied on these two pages, taking their shapes and the materials they are made from into account.

Flat brushes have long bristles and a square point. They are most appropriate for applying or diluting colors that cover wide areas (fig. 1). Used flatly they paint long fluid colors. Used sideways the mark is much thinner and denser. Brushes with a similar shape to flat ones but with shorter bristles are ideal for pasting colors and creating textural effects (fig. 2). Brushes with rounded bristles are more versatile and can cover large areas of color, working with soft strokes and applying pastes quickly (fig. 3). Small ones are ideal for introducing drawings at the first stage and painting details. Filberts are a mixture of flat and round brushes (fig. 4) whose shape gets narrower to end in a curved point, which makes the brush easier to handle. They are perfect for makes thin strokes or for merging and softening contours.

Fanned brushes, made of sable or badger fur, are used for merging two or three colors on the painting surface and for making soft tonal gradations (fig. 5). These merging effects were once created with a feather.

For oil painting resistant horsehair bristles are used just as much as sable ones. Horsehair ones are strong enough to work on a textured surface. They are excellent for painting colored strokes in which the pattern of the brush is left visible on the canvas. Sable bristles, on the other hand, are softer and more fragile for use with oils and thus less resistant. However, they are very useful for making finishing touches and adding details to diluted colors. Soft bristles should only be used for painting delicate areas and never for mixing colors. Synthetic bristles are a cheap alternative to sable ones. They are more resistant and easier to clean, although

Figs. 1 to 5. Here are the different types of brush: flat or squared brush with long bristles (fig. 1), flat or squared brush with short bristles (fig. 2), rounded brush (fig. 3), filbert (fig. 4) and fanned brush (fig. 5)

6A

6B

the cheaper varieties tend to lose their shape more easily than natural ones.

In any case, most brushes are available in a wide range of sizes that are cataloged from 0 to 16. Here is a basic summary of the ones that you will need to start painting. To begin with, you need four horsehair brushes: a number 10 filbert and another number 4, a flat number 10 brush and a rounded number 6, and a soft brush for drawing, the most appropriate would be a soft, nylon number 3. Starting with this selection, you can go on to acquire more brushes according to your particular needs.

Now you should explore the range of strokes that these brushes can produce. The object of this exercise is to familiarize yourself with each one. That way you will feel more confident when you have to choose the right brush for any given task.

7

Fig. 6 (A, B, C, D and E). Here are the stokes and effects that each different brush produces: filbert brush (A), flat brush with long hair (B), fanned brush (C and D) and squared brush with short hair (E). These stokes can be scribbled quite randomly, and then taken as references when you come to paint a picture.

Fig. 7. It is important to have a wide range of different brushes and types of bristles, so that you can vary the effects that are included in each painting.

Care for your Brushes

It does not matter if a beginner uses amateur or professional paints to begin with, but you should always be sure of using quality brushes. Mixing colors with dirty brushes that still contain the remains of previous efforts will eventually spoil your colors, particularly when they are applied in small quantities. It is extremely important that we take proper care of our brushes if we want to make decent paintings.

Therefore, after each session, we need to clean our brushes thoroughly. First, remove any excess paint with a cloth or a piece of newspaper. You will need about an eighth of a page of a normal sized newspaper (fig. 4). Now soak the brush in thinners or turpentine and rub the bristles hard against the cloth. Repeat the process until the brush leaves no mark at all. Then wash the brush in water, scrubbing it thoroughly with a bar of everyday soap (fig. 2). Repeat the process as many times as necessary until there is absolutely no sign of color in the soapsuds (fig. 3). Now rinse the brush in hot water and dry the bristles with a towel. You have not finished until they are all back in their original shape.

You can put off having to wash them by leaving them to soak in a dish of water. But don't get into the habit of doing this, only do so when you have no other choice. If you leave them too long and the stains of paint dry out, there is a product you can buy called Lavapin that can get rid of them. But not only is this a tedious process, it ends up destroying the bristles.

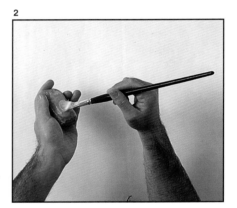

Fig. 1. You can buy metal pots that keep the brushes dipped in thinners, which stops the bristles from losing shape.

Figs. 2 and 3. After painting, you need to wash your brushes. You need to do this when the paint is still fresh. First remove the paint with thinners and a cloth, and then wash the brushes with soap and water until you have got rid of any excess color.

Fig. 4. It is important that you take proper care of your brushes if you want to paint decent pictures.

Painting Supports

The support is the base onto which the painting is applied. For oil painting, it cannot be a porous surface and most have enough fibers to retain the paint. So, if the support needs it, a preparatory layer or primer can be applied before you start painting. This is a thin film of agglutinate or color. However, you should always dedicate a little time to choosing the right support. Although it shouldn't be difficult to find one that is suitable for painting, because practically any material is fine for oil painting, you should understand the characteristics of the three most commonly used supports.

Wood. Paintings on wood are often called boards. As wood is a hygroscopic material (i.e. one with a capacity for absorbing humidity from the atmosphere and exhaling it), it can easily curve out of shape. So wood needs to be prepared before you paint on it. The surface should be flat and smooth, for which a preparatory layer is applied, fundamentally based around plaster. This primer acts as a support for the paint and isolates the humidity and the microorganisms on the reverse side (fig. 1).

Cardboard or paper. These are the most fragile supports of the three because they bend with the application of paint, and therefore need to be applied to a rigid support (fig. 1). Oils applied to these materials lose color and a certain amount of resistance. If, rather than stiff cardboard, you prefer paper, make sure it is consistent and thick enough. If not, the paper will start wrinkling and curling over. Thick, good quality paper is perfect for making small sketches, particularly if you are working outdoors.

Canvas. The most commonly used support for oil painting (fig. 2). Not only does it have a pleasant, natural texture, but it is also light and easy to carry. This textile support is usually made of flax, cotton or hampen cloth. The material comes fitted to its own support; a frame made of strips of wood that are joined at the corners. Nowadays, you will usually find that canvases are already prepared when you buy them. The substance that covers the material closes the pores and isolates the paint, acting as a kind of simple primer.

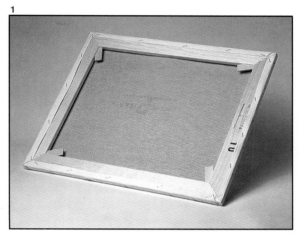

Fig. 1. If you want to paint on paper, medium and thick grain sheets are most appropriate, although you would be better off using cardboard. Oil paints stick to more or less any rigid surface, but boards are best for making sketches and preparatory drawings. You can use a board by priming it or covering it with a cloth.

Fig. 2. Canvases are undoubtedly the best supports for oil painting, and can be used to paint large pictures comfortably. Nowadays, most canvases are already primed when they are sold, and you can paint directly onto them.

Initial Colors: The Outline Sketch

The outline sketch involves all of the initial lines that are applied to the definitive support, the first colors that determine the fit of the image and a rough tonal evaluation of the picture. The first layers of dissolved paint condition the overall effect and final image of the painting.

The first applications of paint determine how the paint is going to stick to the surface and whether it will dry properly without cracking up. There are several ways of doing this:

— Dry drawing. You can paint dry colors by reducing the amount of oil in the mixture and then using a brushload of thick paint to sketch the subject with rough lines that establish the general proportional relationships and determine the fit (fig. 1). The drawing should be made with a neutral color (blue or brown depending on the chromatic tendency of the model).

— Transparent background. Made by covering the surface with paint diluted in thinners. This technique does tend to leave a few paint marks on the sup-

Fig. 1. The first layer of color should be dry. You should use a small brush with a small amount of scarcely diluted paint and merely insinuate the subject with thin lines. It should be a linear interpretation of the subject.

Fig. 2. Some artists prefer an opaque background to a white one, because it tends to be less inhibiting. If you wish to do the same, you have two options. The first involves covering the background with fast-drying acrylic paint and the second involves doing the same but with oils. For the latter you will need to prepare the surface beforehand so that the background is dry before you start painting.

Figs. 3 and 4. The subject can be outlined using an initial tonal evaluation. The subject is composed using plain washes that do not differ too much from the local color of the subject.

port due to gravity and fluidification.

— Opaque tonal background. As a white background can look inhibiting and some artists prefer to use a colored one, you can cover the whole surface with a tonal background color. By covering the whole area with a single color, be it light or dark, you will have a more pleasant background to paint on (fig. 2).

— Chromatic areas. Another system is that of starting by spreading wide areas of a diluted color that define the chromatic areas that the painter has in mind. This involves simplifying and deciding on the general areas of color, designating one to each of the areas in which one particular tone or tendency predominates over any others (figs. 3 and 4).

— Opening lights. A layer of color can be applied over the whole surface of the cloth so as to cover it entirely. Then, by rolling a piece of old cloth around your finger, you can clear areas of paint and outline the subject that way (fig. 5).

— Acrylic base. This is achieved by painting a latex background, or using acrylic paints, to assure fast drying. Once the first outline has dried, you can paint over it with oils as part of the same session.

When you work on a white surface, the transparency of paint over the white background can help with the tonal evaluation. Work by leaving the white of the background more visible wherever the elements of the model are more illuminated (figs. 6 and 7).

The tonal evaluation of the initial colors involves making a simple oil sketch and then establishing the most important features and the tonal gradation of the subject.

The important thing about your outline sketch is that the initial indications should be light, fluid and at the very least, thin. You do not want to create too great a stability or autonomy before you have painted the next layers.

Having reached this point, you must be warned of one thing. Don't think that just because you have painted the outline that the picture is now completely set up. The painting needs to develop as you work, and new problems need to be faced and overcome as you go along.

5

6

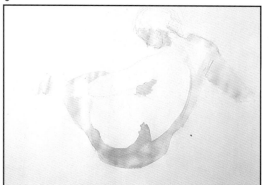

Fig. 5. Cover the background with a uniform wash of paint mixed with thinners and take a cloth to open spaces over the most brightly-lit areas of the subject.

Figs. 6 and 7. In these two illustrations, we can see that the artist has decided to use the white of the paper to show the most brightly-lit areas. This technique is quite common when using oils as washes of paint diluted in thinners.

7

Fig. 1. An understanding of technique is vital for painting an alla prima *landscape like this* View of a peasant's house *by Óscar Sanchís (artist's private collection).*

OIL PAINTING TECHNIQUES

Because they are so malleable, oils can be used for more diverse techniques and methods of representation than any other painting procedure. They are so consistent that the artist can take advantage of the whole scope of the color of his paste.

In the next chapter we will cover all of the most common techniques used in oil painting such as veiling, dry brush painting, using the spatula and wet on wet. We will also look at others, which, though less common, are also of interest. These include incision and scratching techniques, wet white, granulation and painting with the anticerne effect. These subjects are rarely covered in a book like this.

Painting with Veils or in the "Venetian Style"

Oils are one of the procedures that are most suited to the use of veils – thin layers of transparent paint. The effect is very different to that achieved by mixing pastes. When light penetrates the transparent film of the canvas or paper, the painting is clearly illuminated. Two painters from Venice were the first to use the new technique. They modeled the surface of their paintings by superimposing very thin layers, playing with these layers and pastes to accentuate the most brightly-lit areas. That is why the veiling technique is also sometimes called the "Venetian Style".

The bottom tone of a veil is generally the lightest (such as, for example, the white of the paper) and the transparent layer applied over it gives it color, and darkens it at the same time. The basic theory behind adding veils is the modification of the color beneath through transparency (figs. 3 and 4). We use a soft brush so that the brushstrokes are not visible. The thinness of the upper layer makes the color under the veil translucent, lending a shiny appearance to the piece. Before applying a veil, the layer beneath needs to be dry. If you apply a veil onto a fresh base, the colors of the two layers will mix together and dirty each other, destroying the effect of transparency. Therefore, one of the drawbacks of working with veils is the time it can take, so it is a good idea to use Dutch varnish to speed up the drying process.

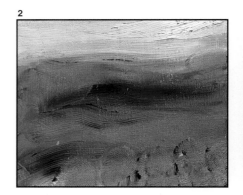

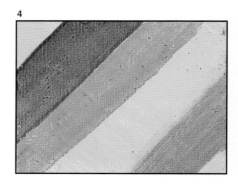

Fig. 1. **Study of a nude** *or* **Susana sewing** *by Paul Gaughin (Ny Carlberg Glyptotek, Copenhagen). A painting that, in order to show the qualities of the skin, uses veils intensively.*

Figs. 2, 3 and 4. Study these different ways of using veils. Above, a soft wash applied on wet (fig. 2), and below, two examples of superimposed colors. In the first illustration (fig. 3), four differently colored diagonal strips are superimposed over an orange background, while in the other illustration (fig. 4), three more strips of color are superimposed over an ochre yellow background. Veiling involves modifying the background through transparency.

The color that is used for applying a veil requires the use of a lot of medium and less pigment (walnut oil is most transparent and therefore the most recommendable for painting veils). The old Masters worked veils with their fingers or the palms of their hands, or sometimes they would use a cloth a cloth, to get softer transitions. It is a good idea to make veils with resins or a little turpentine and thickened oil added, because pure oil can be rather greasy and oily varnishes even more so.

Another possibility is to add a little white to all the tones of a veil because, although it does not spoil the effect of a painting, it does help to conserve it from cracking.

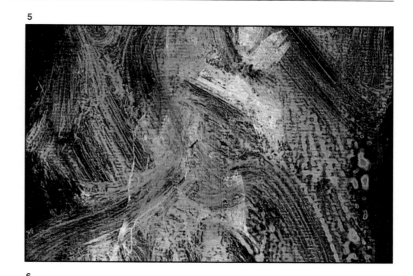

Fig. 5. Oil paintings are sufficiently opaque for superimposing light veils over dark ones. Don't forget that the idea of painting over a dark background is not particularly common for oil painting.

Fig. 6. A section of **The gleaners** *by Jean-François Millet (Louvre Museum, Paris). It is quite common to paint distant planes with merged and veiled colors, creating a sensation of interposed atmosphere.*

Fig. 7. **Still life of cushions** *by Teresa Trol (artist's private collection). Veiling gives a painting a vaporous, almost magical, feel. In this piece, veiling techniques are combined with sgraffito.*

Scraping Techniques

Scraping techniques involve rubbing the bristles of a brush loaded with thick paint along the rough surface of the support (it is important to put the right amount of paint on your brush or you might cover too much of the background and not quite get the right effect).

Dry painting techniques involve a wiry, granulated brush and only cover part of the color beneath. Oil paint sticks to the raised texture of the paper or canvas and creates a dry, grainy sensation. The result of a dry stroke makes oil paint more expressive and is used to suggest different surfaces such as, for example, the roughness of a rock covered in moss, thick vegetation, the foam of the sea as it strikes against a cliff, the texture a porcelain vase, the sand on a beach or the soft fur of an animal.

Blurring is closely related to the use of the dry brush. It is also done with dry tones, although only half-covering, giving a lighter effect and implying the use of less material to complete a picture (blurring is usually

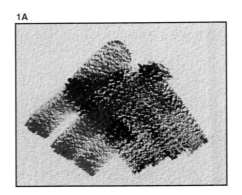

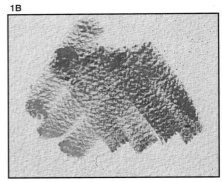

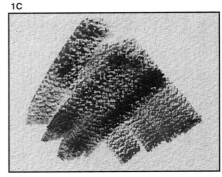

done with thick paint, but diluted paints can also be used). The color underneath the blurred area will show through. To practice this technique, load your brush and remove any excess paint. Paint with circular movements over a surface you have painted beforehand. Rub lightly over the surface with a sponge to soften the texture and merge the tones. The most important thing about this technique is not covering the previous color completely but to leave it visible beneath the superimposed strokes.

You can create interesting effects by blurring the paint with a piece of cloth

Figs. 1A, 1B and 1C. In these tests, we can see what happens when paint is applied to the paper with a dry and granulated brush. We can also see how, just like with veils, colors can be superimposed to create new effects and fusions.

Fig. 2. Here is a **Landscape of a mountain** *by Óscar Sanchís (artist's private collection) using the dry brush technique. Notice how the artist has used the blue color of the paper to great effect, letting it show through the gaps in the paint.*

or tissue paper instead of just using a brush. In the same way, your own hands can be useful tools for smearing the colors. For example, by moving your index finger and thumb either back and forwards or in circular movements, you can blend colors directly onto the support. By merging, these colors mix homogeneously and the overall effect is somewhat satinated and adds impact to chiaroscuro paintings. Both the dry brush and blurring techniques can be used in conjunction because, as I have already explained, the two methods are very closely related.

Figs. 3A and 3B. Look at how different colors are merged to make a tonal degradation. Exercises like this are extremely useful for getting to know the reactions of colors and learning how to blur and merge them.

3A

3B

4

Fig. 4. **Young girl with a basket on her head** *by William Hogarth (National Gallery, London). If you look closely at the girl's face, you will notice how the shadows merge together softly. This technique involves rubbing the brush across the paint so that the edges are less defined and the lines more vaporous*

5

Fig. 5. **Mountain landscape** *by Pablo Picasso (Picasso Museum, Barcelona). In this early painting by Picasso, the paint has been applied freely and skillfully, creating a blurry interpretation of the subject.*

Painting with a Spatula

The spatula is a utensil that includes a wooden handle and a blade made of forged steel to make it more resistant, flexible and easy to use. It is an excellent tool for pasting mixtures of colors, and also for spreading paint over canvas, for rubbing, and for outlining. The movement of the spatula for pasting or mixing paint on the palette is a continuous movement of pressing, going back and forth, scraping or making circles. It can be used not only for mixing certain quantities of paint, but also for slowly adding small amounts of color to adjust different shades. Using spatulas for mixing paint is a good way to avoid spoiling your brushes.

Spatulas, apart from being used for mixing colors, can also be used for applying paint directly to the canvas. They can substitute brushes to create all kinds of effects. Spatulas for painting have shorter blades and their handles are crank shaped to stop them accidentally touching the paint when they are applying color. Paint, when applied with a spatula, comes into contact with the surface in a different way to when it is applied with a brush. Many artists use a spatula to move paint on the surface and this way they can create different textures and details. The edges of the paint are much more defined than those created with a brush. Because they are not so easy to handle as a brush, there is a certain random element to using a spatula, which many artists find stimulating.

If you want to paint a rich, textured surface, you can paint a whole picture using only a spatula. Use the flat base of the blade to paint plain smooth surfaces, and use the pointed end in an energetic way to get rough, pointed structures. Try holding the spatula at different angles, and vary the amount of pressure you apply to create different lines and effects. You will find that spatula work offers all kinds of interesting and

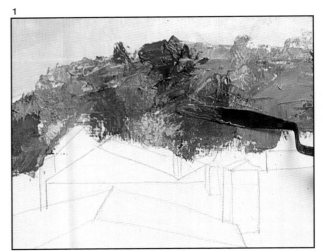

Fig. 1. To work with a spatula you need to take maximum advantage of the flexibility of the blade and of each hand movement. You will eventually be able to form the paint into visible shapes on the surface of your painting.

Fig. 2. Spatulas are not only used for mixing colors on the palette, for eliminating impurities or for removing color. You can also paint with them. In fact, many painters prefer to use spatulas to distribute color and work it into the surface.

Fig. 3. Leman Lake and Grammont Peak by Gustave Courbet (old Brame et Lorenceau collection). Notice how the artist has painted the water with brushes, but combined his work with the use of spatulas to apply the pastes that make up the snow-capped mountains.

effective possibilities. The uninformed tend to scoff that painting with paste is just something for artists to do for a bit of fun. These people do not realize that there are certain lights and textures that can only be created with pasty colors and they confuse the technique with colorist ideas. Not that the spatula should only be associated with pastes — it can also be used for etching, making translucent forms and adding delicate details. The pointed end can also be used for sgraffito.

You will almost certainly find that, at least in principle, it is much harder to paint with a spatula than with brushes, so you will need to practice before you can work freely.

You can buy spatulas in all kinds of shapes and sizes. Choices are generally based on individual preferences.

4

Figs. 4, 5 and 6. In this sequence of three illustrations, you can see the results of spatula work. The first washes can be applied with a brush (fig. 4). Then, using the side of a spatula, the widest areas are defined (fig. 5) and with a smaller one the textures and effects are created (fig. 6). As you can see, you cannot reach high levels of detail with a spatula. The finished picture tends to be rather somber and not particularly detailed, but at the same time, highly effective.

5

6

Opaque Color Techniques

The opaque color technique allows for the superimposition of different strokes without the need to mix colors by merging, degrading or blurring. The directions of the strokes and the pastes applied by the brush play a far more important role. Delacroix used to say that that in the opaque color technique "the painter should model with color as a sculptor would do with clay". Paint is used directly from the tube, or maybe diluted a little, with a touch of medium to make it more malleable, but still dense enough to conserve the lines and strokes, Colors are merged by superimposing and the density of the color leads to greater brightness and contrast between the different areas of color.

Oil is an opaque paint, which implies that light colors can be applied over darker ones. If it is very thick and dry it can completely cover a color. The same chromatic harmony made with light colors can be achieved by superimposing dark ones, which is ideal for painting shadows. The opacity of the color helps work on colored paper. If you work on a colored surface, you will find it easier to value, because you will find it just as easy to apply both light and dark colors right from the start. Remember that opacity varies considerably between different pigments. If you want to increase the opacity of a color, do so by adding white in small quantities, because otherwise you would waste a lot of paint to get very average results.

Colors can be applied dry or fresh, one over the other, neither worrying too much about details nor mixing them on the palette. If you use opaque tones, your brushstrokes will show through clearly and therefore the artist's hand. When painting with opaque colors, maximum advantage is taken of the direction of each stroke, with color and textures being indicated by these strokes and the superim-

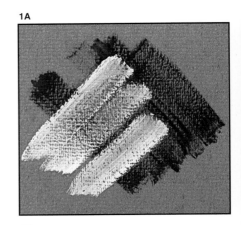

1A

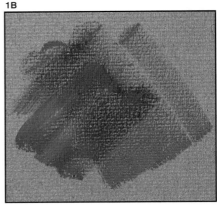

1B

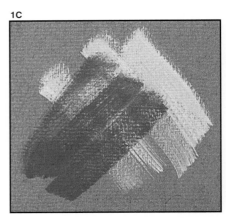

1C

2

Figs. 1 (A, B, C). Strokes of oil paint can be superimposed one on top of the other as many times as we feel necessary. You can check the opacity of a color by superimposing light ones onto dark ones and viceversa.

Fig. 2. **House in the Valle de Arán** *by Josep Antoni Domingo (artist's private collection). As you can see from this painting, the opaque painting technique involves the use of a medium brush pasted with paint to create a painting surface that does not let the background color or that of lower layers to show through, as is the case with veils.*

position of colors and forms. Cool sections alternate with warm ones, and cool tones with warm ones, working together to show the material application of color and at the same time creating harmony. The veiling technique, as was explained before, can be used in conjunction with opaque layers of paint, as long as the latter are dry to the touch. Veils are usually applied as thin washes over the finished piece to gently modify the earlier colors, softening contrasts and harmonizing colors.

As in the previous cases, it is always a good idea to practice on a separate piece of paper.

Fig. 3. **Woman at the window** *by Edgar Degas (Courtauld Institute Galleries). Opaque paint allows painting from dark to light, in other words, preparing a dark background and then gradually adding light. We can see this process in this unfinished piece of work by Edgar Degas.*

Fig. 4. **The red tower at Halle** *by Ernst Ludwig Kirchner (Folkwang Museum, Essen). The artist has worked with dense, opaque, pasted paints. This gives more body to the subject.*

Wet on Wet

This is any technique in which colors are applied to an area of wet paint and when they are spread over the surface and mixed, they form irregular contours.

We apply a small quantity of diluted paint and spread it relatively freely over the surface. While it is still wet, we paint a thicker layer over it. You will observe that the color tends to run on the damp surface, creating soft, blurred edges where the paint is thinnest. Although this type of painting produces spontaneous effects, it needs practice and experience to determine the degree of dampness in the lower layer and the amount of paint that is needed to control the fluidity of the paint in the stroke.

To paint on wet you can use any kind of brush, although for painting small shapes, softer ones are preferable, such as those made of sable, loaded with slightly diluted paint so that the color can be applied more softly. You need to make sure the paint does not dilute too much or the overall effect will be too dull and colorless. When you work, you should stick to a limited range of colors and avoid complex mixtures, which take a lot of the spontaneity out of the piece. Likewise, try to avoid using more than two or three colors, or you will produce disappointing results – a paste of colors made up of successive strokes that look too dirty.

In general, this method gives a soft, transparent quality to the forms, and creates a magical atmosphere that cannot be created in any other way. It is one of the most beautiful and expressive ways of using oils and is particularly effective for painting skies and water due to the subtle tonal gradations that suggest the changing appearances of light. For this reason, it was widely used by impressionist painters for portraying natural light. By painting on wet, these artists introduced a suggestive, lively type of stroke that has contributed to the expression of lighting effects and landscape movements.

1

3

2

Fig. 1. The technique of wet on wet works on the same principle as the merging of colors. By applying one color on top of another before it has dried, both merge into forms with imprecise edges.

Fig. 2. The technique of wet on wet and the use of paper as a support do not work well together because paper absorbs too much oil and the paint dries too quickly. If you want to paint wet on wet, you should use a more porous surface.

Fig. 3. A village in the Valle de Arán by Óscar Sanchís (artist's private collection). Painting on wet is perfectly suited to outdoor work and making little color sketches or noting impressions of the landscape because in such cases one does not want to wait for each color to dry.

4

Fig. 4. **Uphill path between grass** *by Pierre-Auguste Renoir (Musée D'Orsay, Paris). If you look at the vegetation, you will see how the strokes blend into the background, which is a typical result of painting when the previous layer is still wet.*

5

Fig. 5. **Fisherwoman's head** *by Joaquín Sorolla (Sorolla Museum, Madrid). The wet on wet technique is not only useful for landscapes, but can also be used for painting figures and portraits.*

6

Fig. 6. **Interior with flowers** *by Teresa Trol (artist's private collection). Notice how the colors tend to integrate and blend into the image. By painting over one color, the brush also affects the one underneath, and they produce this merged effect.*

Painting *Alla Prima*

Painting *alla prima*, or direct painting, developed out of the idea of painting wet on wet. This style of painting is all about impression, a technique that involves doing everything in just one session, working quickly and never going back over what has been done. The artist's skill, quick application and wisely chosen colors are the key to successful alla prima paintings. This painting method rarely involves a preparatory sketch and neither is it normal for the background to be colored.

As the whole painting can be finished in one session with this technique, it is very useful for painting landscapes. It does not require much elaboration; these pictures include very few details. The idea is to try to capture the audacity of the subject by using wide, generous strokes, pastes of color and lively, expressive lines. It is also a good idea to stick to a limited range of colors and avoid the kind of complex mixtures that can take a lot of the spontaneity out of the image.

By working quickly, the artist can mix colors directly onto the support, so each stroke must be applied very deliberately, thinking carefully about ways of keeping the colors clean.

Direct painting was particularly popular in the impressionist era; one of its main exponents was Claude Monet, who painted from nature at extraordinary speeds, frequently applying one color on top of another so that they mixed on the support itself.

Fig. 1. **Alcázar fountain in Seville** *by Joaquín Sorolla (Sorolla Museum, Madrid). Direct painting is all about capturing sensations, immediate impressions, specific lighting conditions and why not even the artist's mood at the time.*

Fig. 2. **Boats on the Seine** *by Alfred Sisley (Courtaud Institute Galleries). Look at the immediacy of the way the clouds and sky have been painted, and the agitated sensation that the brushstrokes give to the image as a whole.*

Fig. 3. **The port** *by Pablo Picasso (Picasso Museum, Barcelona). Gesture and stroke forms are far more important than details in* **alla prima** *painting. Notice how the people are represented in this picture, little more than amalgamations of colored strokes.*

Wet White Technique

The wet white technique is a laborious and rather unusual method (writings on oil painting rarely deal with the subject), and incorporates characteristics that belong to other better known procedures. In a way, it is a combination of pointillist and wet on wet techniques. Just like Divisionism or pointillism, the colors are not mixed on the palette, but in the spectator's eye.

It is indeed a painstaking process. It is done as follows. The painter starts off by covering the background with a dense layer of lead white mixed with varnish resin. Then, while this layer is still wet, it is painted over with a thin, sable brush. The paint is distributed in the form of small dots, with pure colors being applied as thin strokes. The definitive tones and colors are created by superimposing these strokes. The lead white base and the varnish resin result in a painting with the transparency of miniatures and a range of colors not unlike that of pastels, given that pure colors are mixed on the surface of the white that acts as a background. Paintings that use this method are extremely precise and have a unique form of light. Another advantage of this technique is that the paint takes up to two days to dry, and until then it is still flexible and mobile, so the artist has plenty of time for corrections. However, this is not an easy type of painting to touch up.

Fig. 1. By superimposing stokes onto a white background, the colors mix and create tones that resemble those of pastels.

Fig. 2. You do not always have to use a white background; you can also try other light backgrounds such as yellow, pink or sky blue. You just need to remember that the choice of color will have serious repercussions on the chromatic tendency of the piece as a whole.

Fig. 3. **The cypresses at Cagnes** *(National Museum of Modern Art, Paris). Instead of mixing colors on the palette, this technique involves creating colors and tones on the painting surface, superimposing thin pointillist strokes with pure colors.*

Scratching and Incisions

Scratching, incisions or sgraffito (from the Italian *graffiare,* to scratch), is a technique that involves scratching a layer of color with a sharp utensil, so that either the color below or the white of the paper or canvas shows through. It is not really a painting style, but a way of manipulating and altering the paint after color has been applied. This method is particularly appropriate for creating areas that combine texture and drawings.

Different artists use different tools for doing this: sticks, rods, kitchen utensils, penknives, cloths, sponges, fingers and other objects. Different types of line can be opened depending on the instrument we use and the consistency of the paint.

For several years now, a special tool has been marketed for doing sgraffito, incisions and washes on the painting surface. It is a brush with a wooden handle and a wedge-shaped rubber point. It malleability permits all kinds of effects, depending on the angle of

1A
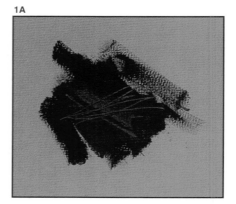

1B
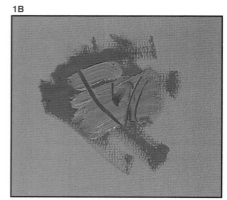

1C
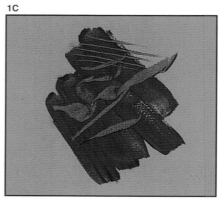

1D
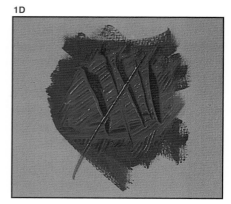

1E
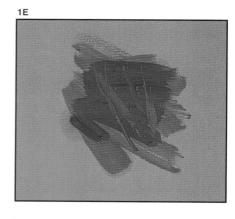

2

Fig. 1. Here are samples of some of the sgraffito effects that can be achieved. If you work directly onto a tonal background, you can get that color back by scraping paint off the surface. If you painted a layer of color underneath, you can use sgraffito to get the color back again.

Fig. 2. In principle, any sharp instrument is fine for sgraffito work. It is always a good idea to try as many different objects as you can on a separate piece of paper to see what effects they produce.

the rubber point and the amount of pressure that is applied. If we scratch a thin enough layer with a jagged instrument, the lines will be thin and hard. On the other hand, if we scratch a thick, damp layer with a blunt instrument, the lines will be less precise and their edges will be slanted. This can be an effective way of expressing the details of a landscape. The bark of a tree, a leafy mass of vegetation, the branches of a bush or the thin, linear touches of light on grass can all be represented by scratching the paint, when it is still wet, with a sharp instrument, such a scalpel, Stanley knife, the reverse end of a brush, a fingernail (it is said that William Turner's little finger had a longer nail than any of the others for scratching light into his paintings) or even a razor blade. Be careful not to damage the actual support by pressing too hard, and work softly and gradually.

When scratching, any mistake can easily be covered up by spreading the color with a spatula or brush, and you can keep practicing sgraffito ideas until you are happy with the result. As oil paint gets hard when it dries, it is not a good idea to scratch dry paint. You would only be damaging the surface of the paint and the results are unlikely to be very satisfactory.

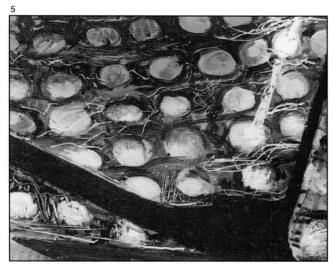

Fig. 3. **Composition with houses** *by Óscar Sanchís (artist's private collection). This is a monochrome painting in which a rubber point has been used to open white spaces. Depending on the angle of the point, either thick or thin openings can be made.*

Fig. 4. The rubber pointed pencil is one of the latest innovations in the world of painting. It can be used on the painting surface to produce all kinds of sgraffito effects.

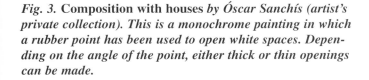

Fig. 5. In this section of a piece by Teresa Trol, we can see how she has used sgraffito techniques.

Fig. 6. **The pretenders** *by Gustave Moreau (Moreau Museum, Paris). This French symbolist was one of the earliest modern artists to make extensive use of incisions in his work.*

Textures with Marble Powder

If we mix latex (a milky looking gum) with marble powder, we get a pasty, cement-like solution that can be applied to the surface of the canvas to create textures and irregular surfaces. The procedure involves thickening and adding volume to the surface, creating a clumsy, irregular appearance with crests and gaps that light and shadow play upon. Ground marble is made up of rough grained lime, practically insensitive to water, that has been used in painting since ancient times. It is often extracted by pulverization, using rotating metal brushes.

With spatulas and brushes with resistant bristles, we make the textures that we need for composition with this paste. The pastes are either light or deep depending on how much of the marble mixture is applied to the canvas. The support must be laid out flat on a table when the marble powder is applied. Once the paste has been applied, it is usually left to dry for a few hours. When the surface is hard, you can paint on it as you would on any other support. It is important that the paste has dried properly before you paint onto it or your brushes will damage the texture that you have spent so much time trying to perfect.

If you have applied thin layers of marble powder, there is a very good chance that it will be ready within two or three hours. However, if you have spread out generously thick layers, I would not advise you to start painting for at least a whole day.

Fig. 1. Latex is a milky substance that, when mixed with marble powder, creates a thick paste that can be applied to any support to create textures and irregular surfaces.

Fig. 2. When it is being prepared, marble paste looks gray. It will regain its white appearance once it has dried.

Fig. 3. While the paste is still wet it can be manipulated and applied to the support. You can prepare the texture that you are going to paint with oils.

Fig. 4. Notice that the characteristic texture in this **Landscape of Cadí** *by Gabriel Martín (artist's private collection) is produced by a marble powder background.*

You will see that when you apply the paste it looks rather grayish when it is still wet, but when it dries out it will be whiter. You can rework marble paste while it is still wet, but once it is dry there is nothing you can do to change things. The only way of modifying it then would be to prepare more paste and spread it over the first layer. Marble powder can be applied to any type of support because latex has very powerful adhesive qualities. However, there is another way of creating textures with marble powder. If you mix colors with marble powder on your palette, you can then apply it to the support with a spatula. The oil paint itself acts as an agglutinate and fixes the mixture onto the surface of the painting.

Whenever you work with marble powder, remember to use synthetic or horsehair bristles, because a surface textured with this material can wear your brushes extremely quickly. There is little doubt that you are probably best off using a spatula for the task. If you use sable brushes, you will find, to your dismay, that they will be destroyed by the granulated marble powder surface.

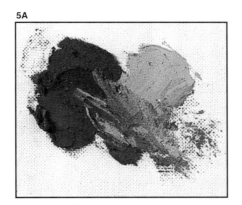
5A

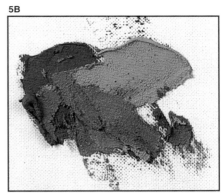
5B

6

Figs. 5A and 5B. Oil paints can be mixed with marble powder on the palette, creating a thick, dense appearance.

Fig. 6. Window by Óscar Sanchís (artist's private collection). This whole piece was painted with oil and marble powder pastes. The paint was applied with a spatula instead of ruining a set of brushes.

Fig. 7. If you are going to paint with brushes, they need to have strong, resistant bristles. Nevertheless, I would strongly recommend that you use a spatula rather than risk spoiling your brushes.

7

Scribbling Technique

In modern painting, the application of covering and corporeal colors plays an important role, and they can be used to create pleasant material effects and excellent qualities and luminosity. As opposed to opinions in the past, it is now often considered beneficial if the strokes are visible, and if the artist's scribbling can be seen on the paper, it can be one of the most attractive aspects of a painting. Shaky, agitated lines can turn a painting into an amalgamation of rhythmic lines that can produce an extraordinary sense of movement in the image.

To paint with this technique you need to observe the internal rhythms of the subject and understand how the external forms respond to this movement. Try to use scribbling to capture, in a cloud of fast but accurate lines and with little apparent direction, the energy that the subject suggests.

By doing this, clouds can be painted with nervous pastes of white color; the sea with wide strokes and somewhat wavy lines that describe the irregular surface of the water; the texture of foliage can be built up with narrow, deliberate lines that simulate the movement of the leaves... And if you want to paint rain, try to insinuate its effects with diagonal lines over a thick layer of paint. The use of scribbling is particularly appropriate for painting the elemental forces of nature, where it is hard to portray such a transitory nature without losing the sense of movement. In such cases, do not try to freeze the moment; use the scribbling technique to produce an impression of movement and fluidity. Work on the surface with regular shades that you apply with the edge of your brush. To create thicker textures and clearer marks, press down harder.

When you draw from nature, be brave and work on the rhythm of the movement of each element. When you find a subject that makes your adrenaline flow, paint it at that very moment if you can. Scribbling is an excellent way of making small landscape sketches,

1A

1B
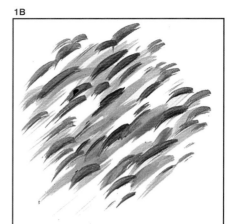

2A

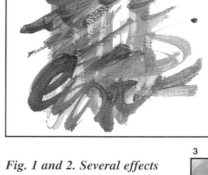

2B

Fig. 1 and 2. Several effects can be achieved with scribling. Try to discover them for yourself by making little tests on a separate sheet of paper. Try to vary your lines and superimpose different colors.

3

Fig. 3. **Mountain in Solius** *by Grau Carod (artist's private collection). The way in which energy is captured and the inherent dynamism of the subject depend to a large degree on the correct pose and the vitality of the lines and strokes.*

miniature impressions that are filled with a strong expressionism. The unexpected and the artist's personality will be much more memorably portrayed this way, and it is often better to leave artistic creation to instinct and to let the brush itself dictate or ignore established rules as it produces paintings as attractive as the one we have included on these pages.

*Fig. 4. **The Emperors** by Van Gogh (Cleveland Museum of Art). The scribbling technique, although less refined, gave the Dutch artist Vincent Van Gogh the perfect medium for underlining the dramatism of these century old trees.*

*Fig. 6. **Don Quijote and Sancho Panza**, by Honoré Daumier (Kuntshalle, Zurich). Scribbling is used here to lend the scene a certain dramatism and dynamism.*

*Fig. 5. **Autumn on the plains of Cadí**, by Gabriel Martín. The use of scribbling in painting involves painting small, shaky lines and pastes that describe the volume of a landscape as best they can.*

The *Anticerne* Effect

Anticerne is a technical term that is used to refer to a way of painting in which the contours allow the color of the support to breathe between different areas of color, so that the color of the support or the background color play an integral role in the piece. This was an extremely popular method in the fauvist era.

Letting background tones and colors show through the paint highlights intensity and the spectacular qualities of color, as well as harmonizing a picture chromatically. Certain colors have discordant relationships – they oppose each other and create visual vibrations.

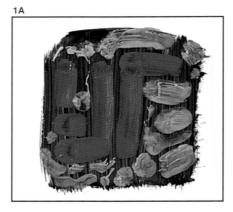

1A

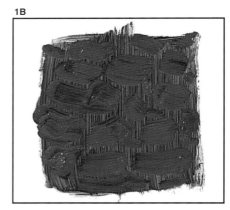

1B

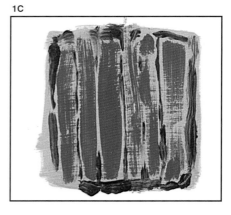

1C

This way, by juxtapositioning two complementary colors (the background and the paint) with the same intensity, strident visual effects can be achieved. In general, we can say that a color appears weaker when it is placed next to a more intense one, and stronger if it is placed next to its complementary. These effects are most apparent where the two colors meet, so to get the maximum stridency; large spaces should be left where the background color shows through. The *anticerne* effect exploits this to a maximum. The treatment of color when using *anticerne* ideas is based on the need to transmit the energy, vitality and strength that the artist is feeling.

The more you know about color, the better you will be able to control its effects. The best way of finding out about the way colors behave under the *anticerne* effect is to try out tests on separate pieces of paper. Experience, observation and experimentation will help you to improve your knowledge.

2

Fig. 1 (A, B and C). In these small color tests the artist has chosen a background color and studied the visual sensations that are produced by the juxtaposition of different color pairs.

Fig. 2. This painting by Óscar Sanchís, Barcelona port (artist's private collection), is a beautiful example of the exuberant use of color that the anticerne effect characterizes. Notice how the color of the paper shines through the strokes of paint, creating an exciting chromatic vibrancy.

Granulation

This is an effective way of suggesting textures like sand. The technique involves loading your brush with paint that is not too liquid and spreading it over the canvas by softly tapping it with the point of your brush. Use separate strokes and don't concentrate your efforts too much on any given area. Don't put too much paint on your brush, or the results will look too pasty. To avoid this problem, keep a piece of newspaper in your other hand to remove any excess paint.

Colors are mixed on the actual support, so that the tones create colors through pointillism and granulation by means of the delicate and careful application of small marks, to portray the effect of corporal separation of light on a landscape. This way you will be able to superimpose the number of colors that you want without taking the freshness out of your painting. The best brushes for the task are cheap ones with rounded, synthetic bristles, because repeatedly pressing the bristles onto the support will wear them out in just a few sessions.

This method is closely related to pointillism and creates a definite sense of unity in a piece, with an atmospheric effect that is hard to obtain with any other technique. It can be combined with other methods – for instance, you could use it to add interest to wide areas of veils and plain colors.

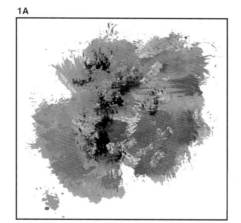

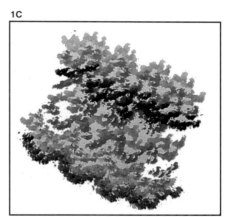

Fig. 1. These are the color tests that the artist Grau Carod made to check the granulation of his brushes, including the way that different mixtures of color behave on paper.

Figs. 2 and 3. Granulation plays an important role in Grau Carod's work. These two sequences give us the opportunity to see how he applied color to a painting called **The path** *(artist's private collection).*

PRACTICAL
EXERCISES

After a brief study of the composition of color, brushes, supports and other accessories needed for oil painting, this book now goes on to show how to apply the techniques explained on earlier pages in a practical way. I suggest that you use the guides that you will find at the back of the book and try each of the following exercises yourself. All of them are based on the work of professional artists. Each exercise is accompanied by a simple, didactic text that you can easily follow systematically. So, turn over the page and get down to work.

Painting a Still Life with Dry, Merged Strokes

We are going to start the second half of this book with a very simple exercise – painting a still life using the dry brush technique. As its name suggests, this technique involves the use of barely diluted paint, whereby color is applied to the grainy roughness of the support. The best kinds of strokes for the task are flat, because they produce the widest and most vigorous marks. This exercise is going to follow the steps of an artist called Carlant. Take a sheet of card, canvas or primed board and do as the artist does. The model is a simple still life of fruit, silver cups and ceramic objects, all with different colors and textures (fig. 0)

Before starting, the artist has decided on the composition of the elements that he is going to paint. Play around with the layout of your still lives before deciding on the most attractive arrangement. You might place them intuitively, but as you observe your arrangement, you should think about Plato's basic rule of "finding unity within variety". An excess of variety can generate a sensation of dispersion, whereas a lack of it can look too forced and monotonous.

Once you have decided on the layout of the elements, start drawing the model, synthesizing the forms and molding the main details (fig. 1). Notice how the artist has depicted the folds of the cloth with a few simple lines. You should do the same.

The first thing to worry about is the construction of the forms with colored strokes that can then progressively be made to resemble the model more. Paint the jug with a mixture of burnt umber and gray. For the apples in the bowl, use carmine, and for the rest of the fruit, dark cadmium yellow with a little ochre. This same ochre should be added to the fruit bowl (fig. 2). Notice that when he paints these initial colors, the artist is already starting to add volume and shadow to the objects. Start painting the background to draw the image together as a whole. This is painted with gray gradations that lead from violet tones to browner ones (fig. 3). Notice that the softer folds have been painted as tenuous gradations of color, while the darker ones are painted with more intense, burnt umber lines.

The artist continues working on the background and the volume and texture of each element. Do the same. Notice how the artist manages to represent the qualities of the materials with strokes and color – the roughness of the ceramic jug, the flat, shiny surface of the glasses and the sinuous waves of the cloth (fig. 4). Once the first phase is complete,

Fig. 0. The model is quite straightforward. It is a simple still life made up of different materials and qualities.

Fig. 1. The composition of a still life is very important. The preparatory sketch is fundamental in representing the model correctly, and will affect the overall appearance of the piece.

Fig. 2. The artist does not work in monochrome. From the very start, he is interested in putting volume into the objects.

Fig. 3. After the first few applications of color, the artist works on the background in a synthetic way.

4

Fig. 4. The first lights are incorporated to highlight each form.

Fig. 5. The dry brush technique allows for superimposed textures, merging and attractive chromatic variations.

the artist steps back to see how everything works in unison, making sure that he has managed to integrate the background and the objects with the right projections of light, shadow and color. Now it is time to accentuate the contrasts and define the forms a little more, working on each object separately, adding color, touching up outlines and projecting shadows (fig. 5).

As the piece progresses, you can see how rich textures can be when we merge colors with the dry brush technique. There is a very definite chromatic harmony and several blurred, sinuous outlines (fig. 6). The artist goes back to the cloth, now with a bigger brush to apply pinker colors and light ochres to suggest the patterns of light more clearly.

To finish, the artist takes a small brush and using short, pasty strokes he accentuates **5** contrasts, the quality of the materials and the reflections and sparkles of light. The painting is now finished (fig. 7).

Fig. 7. The final result is much closer to a realist interpretation of the subject.

6

Fig. 6. At this stage, the details of the painting are much more evident.

7

Landscape with the Pointillist Technique

For this exercise, we are going to be working with the artist Grau Carod, who is going to use pointillism to paint a scene with a waterfall in the midst of a wood. This technique involves applying unmixed paint in short, brightly colored strokes. The exercise will not be done with traditional oil paints, but with water soluble ones. This is a good way of experimenting with new colors, and studying how they tint and dry. If you do not have any, you can still do the exercise with ordinary paints. The artist uses a limited palette: permanent green, emerald green, ultramarine blue, cadmium yellow, cadmium red, carmine, ochre and raw umber (as well as black and white). The artist is going to base his work on this pretty illustration of a waterfall in a wood near Revel in France (fig. 0).

As you can see, the artist is going to work on a dry, tonal background. Do the same. Start by drawing the model with burnt umber and a small brush. You needn't be too precise, but make sure you position the waterfall correctly, along with a few traces of vegetation and the building in the top, right corner (fig. 1). Now take a small brush and start applying small touches of opaque color to the surface of the painting. Start with the sky and the water tumbling over the waterfall. You need to partially cover the vegetation at the edges with white and permanent green dots mixed with a little yellow, and use raw umber and black where the shadows are more intense (fig. 3) As you can see, the artist works on the whole painting at the same time – he mixes one color, applies a few dots and then moves on to a new part of the painting.

Little by little, white disappears from the picture. With a little raw umber, paint the tree trunks and branches and enrich the vegetation with new greens (fig. 4).

Adjacent colors are only mixed in the spectator's eyes when the picture is seen from a distance, so you should keep stepping back a few feet to see how your work is developing. You need to paint in a certain rhythm that always involves checking how everything is coming on. You can elaborate the foreground by spreading new emerald green dots mixed with white, ultramarine blue and violet to represent the water in the stream. The lower part of the painting is comple-

mented with a few irregular ochre lines mixed with a little white (fig. 5).

The waterfall has been developed a little more, and the way the water flows is now clearly shown. New blue dots are gradually starting to suggest the thickness of the vegetation. Small ultramarine blue pastes can be seen in the sky (fig. 6). The colors follow progressively, and as he starts work on details, the artist now uses thinner brushes. Consequently, the chromatic combinations are increasingly richer and more precise. There are touches of two or three colors of very

Fig. 0. The model is this peaceful woodland scene near the French town of Revel.

Fig. 1. The artist constructs the outline sketch with a brush over a tonal background.

Fig. 2. At first, the piece does not look particularly accurate, covered with apparently meaningless dots.

Fig. 3. As his work progresses, the artist adds new values to those of before.

4

5

similar hues next to each other, which mix in the spectator's eyes as completely new ones (fig. 7).

At this stage, the picture as a whole, seen from a certain distance, transmits chromatic sparkles and a shiny, vivacious landscape. The artist has made the foreground denser to show how it differs to the more distant planes. He has done this by combining blues, oranges, reds and ochres in the water of the stream (fig. 8).

Now all that remains is to take a final look over the piece, and as long as you are happy with what you see, you can consider your work finished.

To work with the daring colors of Divisionism, you need a well developed sense of color, but don't feel intimidated. As you try out new combinations and superimpositions, you will find that pointillism is a very easy and satisfying procedure.

6

TIPS

–You sometimes need to exaggerate or reduce colors and forms to make your painting look unified.
–The smaller the dots are, the more surprising the chromatic effects of your paintings will be.

Fig. 7. As the painting nears completion, the artist uses smaller brushes.

Fig. 8. The finished painting shows the kind of complex optical mixtures that can be achieved by superimposing different colors.

7

Fig. 4. At this early stage, the artist has used a medium brush to cover the surface of the painting quickly.

Fig. 5. As you can see, work with pure, clean colors makes pointillist painting extremely bright and gives them a chromatically strident effect.

Fig. 6. After a few hours' work, the painting looks like this. The successions of dots now suggest where the piece is heading.

8

55

Painting a Mountainous Landscape with Veils

In the following exercise, we are going to be using the veiling technique. We shall be working with the artist and illustrator Josep Antoni Domingo. As you already know, veiling involves painting transparent or translucent layers over what has been painted earlier. To manipulate the paint and make the transparency effect stronger, you need to mix it with a veiling medium such as polymerized oil, opium oil or linseed oil thickened in the sun and diluted with turpentine. The color on the palette should be like a glass laminate. That said, we can move on to the exercise.

The model that the artist is going to paint is this mountain landscape dominated by soft tones and sweet contrasts of light and shadow (fig. 0). It is an ideal subject for painting with veils. You will find the preparatory drawing on guide number one. Take it, and paint as the following instructions explain.

First of all, the general distribution and basic outlines need to be established. You need to define how everything fits, using a small rounded brush and a grayish color diluted in a little thinners to scribble the main forms of the model.

Now take a large, flat brush and cover the sky and part of the cliff with a first layer of a gray that you have heavily diluted with thinners. The shadowed parts of the intermediate plane are painted with similar ultramarine blue washes, and the foreground should include a hint of violet. Use wide, heavy brushstrokes for doing all of this (fig. 2)

In a landscape, it is always a good idea to start with the sky. The layer of sky is painted over the pencil drawing, which should now be hidden by these first colors. To paint the sky and the rock faces, a series of plain washes is applied, getting progressively darker to form a light degradation. The rocky mountain is painted with a large, round brush, using a mixture of burnt sienna, ultramarine blue and burnt umber. The strokes are applied upwards and downwards so that they blend into each other. For the sky, you need to make a mixture of cobalt blue, ultramarine blue and titanium white. As there is a lot of sky, it can be painted quickly with either a large, flat brush or a large, rounded one. Pay a lot of attention to the outlines of the clouds, making sure that they blend naturally into the surrounding atmosphere (fig. 3). You will see that the canvas is now completely covered with thin layers of color. The whole painting is full of light and the white of the paper can still be seen through the soft veils. For the greens in the foreground, emerald green, perma-

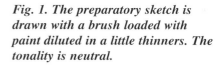

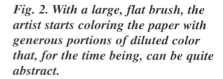

Fig. 0. The subject, a magnificent valley in Huesca, Spain, is dominated by a mountain range with vertical, rocky faces. The clouds project interesting patterns of light and shadow.

Fig. 1. The preparatory sketch is drawn with a brush loaded with paint diluted in a little thinners. The tonality is neutral.

Fig. 2. With a large, flat brush, the artist starts coloring the paper with generous portions of diluted color that, for the time being, can be quite abstract.

Fig. 3. Remembering that the artist uses transparency so that the colors below mix with the washes applied over them, you can see how important tonal effects are in the first washes.

nent green, yellow and cobalt blue have been used. Volume and values have been added through the use of several semi-transparent layers of color. The thin touches of darker color are now added to suggest the texture of the rocky mountain (fig. 4).

At this point, it is a good idea to leave the paint to dry for a few hours. You should really leave it overnight, or even for several days. Remember that whenever you paint with veils, you need to let each layer dry before you paint another over it. If you don't, the colors will mix and destroy the clean lighting effects of the piece. When enough time has passed, you are free to carry on where you left off. You need to work a little more on the contrasts. The artist uses his skill to create an illusion of bright, shining light. One way to do this is to mix the warm, sun-soaked colors that cover the landscape (light greens, ochres, and yellows) with cool blues, grays and violets. Warm colors should look more intense through careful use of contrast. Bear this in mind as you copy the artist (fig. 5).

Now work on the rock faces of the mountains in the background. The texture of the rocks is painted with layers of plain washes. Each wash includes a series of horizontal strokes, one on top of the other. If you look closely, you will notice how the strokes are slightly superimposed over others. So that each stroke stays wet and can be mixed into the next, you need to work fast (fig. 6). With a medium brush, intensify the violets in the foreground to increase the sense of depth in the painting.

With the painting almost complete, apply the point of a small brush with darker touches to reinforce the volume and texture of the rocky mountains. This is the best moment for adding details such as the cracks in the rocks (fig. 7). Dark strokes are applied to the mounds of grass in the middle and foreground, darkening and highlighting the relief and the plays of

4

5

6

Fig. 4. For the moment, you do not need to make your work look too finished, because you still have to cover the hills with more washes.

Fig. 5. The artist has worked on all of the areas of color with veils. The interaction between layers produces a particularly soft, suggestive effect.

Fig. 6. This illustration clearly shows how subtle merging and blurring effects soften the edges of the different areas of color.

light. Strengthen the violet near the rocks in the foreground and touch up the edges of the stream. At this final stage, before you can consider the painting finished, your work must be meticulous and a lot will depend on your observations and the amount of definition that you want there to be in the picture (fig. 8).

Each veil modifies the color of the one before and creates subtle harmony between each tone. Painting veils with a medium like oils, which can involve such long drying times,

can be a laborious process because you need to wait for each layer to dry before you can add another. But if you don't observe this basic rule, the colors will mix and the finished painting will look dirty.

If you add a veil, but then feel that it

is too intense, take a fanned brush, hold it vertically, and brush short strokes over the surface. This will get rid of the excess paint and leave a softer, brighter veil, through which the color beneath will be visible. Another worthwhile alternative is to correct

7

TIPS

–For making veils, it is usually a good idea to choose the largest brush that you can possibly use for each task. This will make the strokes wider and freer.

–To save time, you can paint veils of oil over a background that you have pre-painted with egg tempera, casein, acrylics or non-liquid colors that dry in minutes rather than days.

–Veils should contain paint that is diluted in a special veiling medium to increase its fluidity and transparency.

8

9

Fig. 7. Once you have reached this stage, when the masses of color have been applied, you need to replace your large and medium brushes with small, rounded ones with sable bristles.

Fig. 8. Now it is time for the small, rounded brush to come into play for the final details and to highlight the texture of the rock faces.

Fig. 9. Although work with veils produces a flat effect, its appearance is richer and brighter than when colors are mixed on the palette.

10

mistakes with a shaving brush or any similar type of brush with thick bristles. You can also use a piece of cotton or blotting paper. If areas painted with a uniform veil still need modification, such as clearing areas for touches of light, work on these parts with smaller brushes. The contours and edges of the different areas of color can also be a problem. Different colored veils can be applied to adjoining areas, and they can then be softened and merged to level up the tones and avoid the formation of silhouettes or, to put it a different way, outlines that are too linear or defined (fig. 10).

Fig. 10. The fascinating brightness of the finished piece explains why oil painters are so attracted to the use of veils for painting the effects of outdoor light and atmosphere.

Painting Flowers with Colored Pastes

In this exercise, the artist Teresa Trol is going to show you how to use pasting techniques to represent a floral arrangement, possibly the most popular of all still life themes. As you know, pasting involves applying thick layers of scarcely diluted paint, so that the texture of the strokes is evident on the painting surface. Painting flowers demands a vigorous, colorist treatment. The pasting technique is highly appropriate for this kind of work because of the way it accentuates volume and creates results with a characteristic plasticity.

The artist starts by drawing the subject with charcoal. You will find this drawing on guide sheet number two. You will notice that the artist has opted for a frontal view, with hardly any of the background in sight (fig. 0). She has done this to make the most of the vivacious brightness of the flowers. A floral arrangement, no matter how simple it may be, requires careful layout and composition.

Start working in the same way as Teresa Trol, with accurate, synthetic lines, adjusting proportions and defining forms. Don't worry too much about the particular details of each flower (fig. 1).

Now you can start painting. Start applying a background of ochre diluted in thinners. Vary the proportion to make small degradations and so that the wash does not look too regular. Over this first mixture, when it is still wet, add a pinch of burnt sienna to highlight and silhouette the aura around the edges of the flowers. For the table, use a dark and very diluted green with a touch of ochre added to it (fig. 2).

Now the artist prepares the colors that she is going to use to paint the flowers. As you will have seen in the photograph, this is a warm color range. The artist prefers to work with just a few colors and use them to create the different tones.

So it should be enough to have just cadmium yellow, cadmium red and white on your palette, along with the colors you used for the background. You will be able to use these colors to get all of the rich shades that you are after. Teresa has started constructing the forms with areas of color and pencil lines (fig. 3).

She now makes short, energetic movements to superimpose colors and create volume. You should do the same. Notice how a few touches of white in some flowers help to accentuate shape. At the same time, the artist modifies the treatment of the background to increase the harmony of the piece as a whole.

To show the shadow of the flowers, which is caused by an intense frontal light, darken the left of the background with burnt umber and a touch of black. This will highlight the flowers even better and the picture will seem deeper. To put texture into the table, use freer, more relaxed strokes.

Fig. 0. This is the model that has been chosen for painting. One color usually dominates in floral arrangements. In this case, warm tones contrast on a neutral background.

Fig. 1. Before drawing, the artist observes and analyzes to decide which fit most highlights the characteristics of the subject matter.

Fig. 2. If you mix a few basic colors, you can create a wide variety of tones. By limiting the color scheme, you will avoid too many colors confusing the picture.

Now that much of the painting is done, spend a few minutes studying the picture from a distance, and think carefully about what you have done so far. Remember that a lot of a painter's work goes on in the head. By thinking carefully before doing anything, you will be able to anticipate most of the questions that will come up as you paint.

Now get back to the canvas, and carry on working. Look for volumes, define forms and accentuate contrasts. If you spend a little time studying each flower, you will see that each petal is determined by the shadow of the others – by the tonal contrasts between the same color range. The shadows vary the intensity of the colors and tones (fig. 5). The artist models the texture and form of each flower with the tip of her brush. She exaggerates the plasticity of the leaves with thickly loaded brushstrokes, spreading the color widely and generously. In the leaves, she uses a dark green with a touch of white and dark carmine. She goes on to paint the pot with white and a little blue to show form (fig. 6). You should do the same.

Fig. 3. The direction of the strokes and texture of the surface highlight the vitality of the flowers.
Fig. 4. The colors get more intense and expressive. Tonal contrasts play an important role in such a beautifully balanced composition.
Fig. 5. The artist enriches the background texture. All the parts of the painting are just as important as the actual subject and must come into harmony with the foreground

6

TIPS

–When doing an exercise like this, try to use loose strokes, and don't feel that you always have make an exact copy of the model. A still life needs to be spontaneous and dynamic.

–Try not to go for a perfectly detailed image that lacks life. Flowers are open forms and need to be painted with a certain amount of freedom.

Fig. 6. As the painting progresses, the shadows are developed, forms are molded and everything takes on volume.

Fig. 7. Now is the time for those last pieces of detail that strengthen the result. Use a small, round sable brush for the task.

7

To finish the exercise, work on the details with a thin brush to produce more strength and expressiveness (fig. 7). And here is the finished painting. Notice how such a colorful treatment transmits so much freshness and vitality.

You cannot fail to be impressed by the expressiveness of the piece, and it is the pastiness of the colors that has caused this effect. The artist's work shows how vivid thick, pasty oils can be. You have almost certainly painted all of the flowers in the same way, which is not the right way to go about things. If you look closely, you will see that the larger flowers were painted with pastes on wet, mixing the paint on the surface with the same strokes – what we could call grooved strokes. The daisies are much flatter and more uniform, having been painted with the opaque technique. However, in the centers of some of the flowers, there are small touches of thick paint, which have used all the paint that the brush can hold. The final impression of movement in the painting is associated to the direction and

8

strength of the strokes, always from the center of the flowers outwards. The fact that the background has been worked with darker, plainer colors also contributes to this, centering the interest of the spectator on the most brightly-lit part of the painting, the bunch of flowers (fig. 8).

You may well want to rectify things as you paint. It is very simple – use a spatula to take off any color from the painting surface and then paste over it. You can do this as many times as you like.

Fig. 8. Look at how the artist has kept the spontaneity of her first sketches without forgetting the harmonious effect that the delicacy of floral subjects preserves.

Seascape with the Wet on Wet Technique

0

The wet on wet technique is ideal for outdoor work. It is quite a fast way of painting, with everything being completed in just one session, and paint being applied while that below it is still damp. The direct painting method is technically very safe. Paintings like this, which do not involve any preliminary painting, have an intimacy and freshness that the spectator responds to directly and spontaneously.

We shall start by studying the chosen model – a small cove on the Costa Brava in Spain (fig. 0). Beaches and coves are a great source of inspiration to our invited artist, Teresa Trol. If want to copy her, you should use guide sheet number three at the back of this book.

Once again, the landscape is outlined in the form of a simple drawing – enough to situate the mass of trees, the houses and the beach. The preparatory sketch does not have to be complete, but it should indicate all of the main features (fig. 1).

If you are painting outdoors, you need to mark out every shadow because they are going to change as the day goes by and spoil everything that you have planned to do. Take a large brush for the task, apply a raw sienna wash and indicate where all of the shadows lie. Notice that the initial wash is very free and there are several clear sections where the white of the support is visible, simulating the brightest areas of sun. This way, the image looks three-dimensional. From this simple prelimi-

nary sketch, Teresa elaborates the structure of the piece (fig. 2).

Now it is time to establish the first tonal values. Use a little emerald green for the vegetation, ultramarine blue and cadmium green for the sea, and violet for the shadowed rocks to the left. The artist applies colors to the canvas one on top of the other, diluting them in a little thinners, as if they were

1

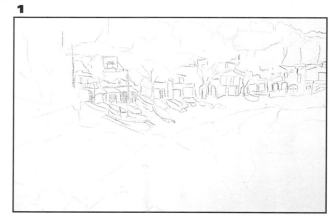

2

Fig. 0. Teresa Trol is going to paint this model, a view of Cala Salguer, a picturesque fishing cove near Palamós, a town on the Spanish Costa Brava.

Fig. 1. The preliminary pencil sketch outlines the forms of the houses and beach.

Fig. 2. A brownish color is used to suggest the positions of the shadows. You will often need to do this when you paint outdoors.

watercolors. As she works, she changes the position of the board to increase or decrease the flow of paint (fig. 3). As you can see, the preparatory sketch is still visible at this stage.

Now work on the group of houses with a small, rounded brush. The doors and windows are painted with two or three superimposed strokes that contrast with the whitewashed walls. The skill of observing an image and translating it to canvas normally only comes with a great deal of practice and almost always involves highly schematic painting methods (fig. 4).

When you paint the houses, you should differentiate the walls by varying the colors and lighting. Use a few strokes of a neutral white, with a little ochre, violet or cobalt blue. Work alla prima, in other words, hardly mix colors on your palette at all, instead letting the wet paints mix on the support itself (fig. 5).

Go around the shadowed area on the left, mixing violet and burnt umber directly on the canvas. In the same way, paint the boats on the sand alla prima. Painting wet on wet in this way is not only technically difficult, but your strokes will intensify any insecurity. But this can actually be used to your advantage, for example when you form the boats, you can make them rough and imprecise. With a small brush, paint the trees between the houses in a similarly imprecise way, using two colors (permanent green and ochre).

The surface of the water is painted with different mixtures of colors – violet and white for the area nearest to the rocks; emerald green, permanent green and cadmium yellow for the central strip; and ultramarine blue and white on the right. Notice that this is not a uniform wash, but several different mixtures and spirited strokes that are superimposed on wet.

3

4

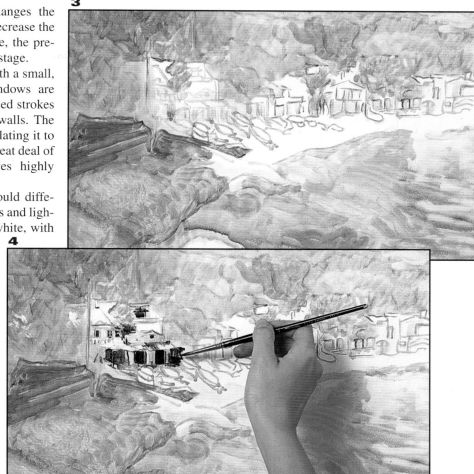

Fig. 3. Successively, the artist fits the composition with the first tonal values painted with very diluted colors.

Fig. 4. With a small brush and thick, dense paint, start detailing the openings in the fishermen's houses.

5

Fig. 5. Now use a small brush to make intense colors, just as they come from the tube, to paint the openings in the fishing huts.

65

6

The color needs to be a bit thick and not diluted too much, or the painting will run too easily. It needs to look slightly pasty (fig. 6). Notice that the strong color of the sea is lighter as it approaches the sunny part of the beach (fig. 7). Remember that when you apply a thick color over another wet one, the brush should be well loaded with paint. If not, all it will do is dirty the color. The foliage adopts an increasingly green color, often with a few yellow and ochre tones. The brushstrokes are overlapped and superimposed. In mid-summer trees look leafier than ever, and the foliage tends to be dark and intense.

7

Fig. 6. Now work on the dark parts of the rocks on the left. The mixture is made up of cadmium red, ultramarine blue and burnt umber.

Fig. 7. To paint the bright reflections on the surface of the sea, the artist applies short strokes with a large, round brush.

Fig. 8. While the paint is still wet, scratch a few light lines with the reverse end of your brush.

TIPS

–The darker brushes contain burnt sienna, and the warmer colors contain more ochre and yellow.
–It is better to mix colors on the palette and paint in zones. Mixtures on the canvas must be meditated to keep the colors clean.
–Some procedures dramatically reduce the strength of some contrasts. One of these is merging wet layers of paint with your finger.

8

9

Taking advantage of the fact that the surface of the canvas is still wet, it is fun to scratch the paint with the reverse end of the brush, making the little twigs that can be seen amongst the green vegetation (fig. 8).

The finished piece has attempted to combine strong contrasts of light in soft harmony. The solidity of the rocks and their structured forms contrast with the continuous movement of the water (fig. 9). It is sometimes hard to capture such changeable effects without losing the sensation of movement. I advise you not to try to freeze the moment, but to make a few measured lines and strokes that produce the impression of movement and fluidity on the surface of the water. I suggest that you do exercises like these in the open air, rather than just copying a photo. This way, although you need to work quickly to capture the moving effects of light, this sense of urgency

will inevitably lead to more vitality in the painting.

When you paint wet on wet, your colors may get altered or dirtied on the surface of the painting. It is not a good idea to manipulate the paint too much once it has been applied. To stop your colors getting muddy, the paint should be on the tip of your brush and your strokes need to be solid and homogenous, the brush held over the damp paint at right angles to the canvas. If you have made a mistake in any one particular area, you can scratch the paint away with a knife, taking out the color and then repainting it while it is still wet. Many artists do this, and what may look spontaneous and flowing may actually be the result of a third or fourth attempt.

Fig. 9. Seascapes like this are extremely popular with artists. Not only do they have a unique quality of light, but there are also just as many pictorial themes as one would find inland.

Landscape with Marble Powder

In this next exercise, we are going to see how the artist Grau Carod goes about painting with the technique of creating textures with marble powder. It will also help you to understand how a fatty medium, such as oil painting, can be mixed with a more acrylic procedure, such as marble powder.

To do this step by step exercise, as well as oil paints, you will need about 250 grams of latex and 300 grams of marble powder. Pour both elements onto a plastic plate or a piece of glass and mix them with a little water to make a paste with a consistency similar to that of cement.

Now study the model. It is a pretty view of Miravet, near Tarragona in Spain, which combines fields and trees, highly appropriate for creating interesting textural effects (fig. 0). Decide how you are going to represent the relief. Do as the artist does: take a spatula and start molding the surface of the support with the paste (the support should be laid out flat on a table) (fig. 1). Try to represent the relief of the vegetation on the mountains with small pastes. Leave one side white, without texture, for the sky and the groups of hills in the distance (fig. 2). Before you start painting, leave the mixture to dry for at least a day.

After that time has passed, pass your hand over the surface to check that it has dried properly and that, consequently, the support is ready to be painted on.

Start painting the sky and the distant hills with ultramarine blue washes with a touch of carmine. The color should be slightly diluted with thinners so that the paint is deposited in the creases and irregularities of the surface. Also, add ochre and permanent green to the more distant planes (fig. 3).

Fig. 0. The model is this pretty view of Miravet, a little village near Tarragona, Spain. Its orography is just right for working with marble powder.

Fig. 1. Use a spatula to apply the marble powder directly onto the support in the right shapes and patterns.

Fig. 2. Compare this image to the original photo and you will see that the relief and pastes of texture are just the same as those in the model.

Fig. 3. Start covering the sky and distant hills in different colors and add the first greens to the vegetation.

With just three or four colors, the artist establishes the compositional layout and sets out the color key. Do the same. Spread more color over the rough surface so that brown and green colors dominate. Permanent green and ochre, in particular, will play an important role in the finished piece. At this point, the artist uses deliberately large strokes to avoid details. This is a useful tactic if you want the paint to have a wide, daring conception (fig. 4).

Here are the first tonal values. They may not be the definitive colors, but they will serve to eliminate the intrusive white of the support. The color has been applied with irregular, slightly blurred outlines. Both the houses and vegetation have been simplified and painted with large areas of color (fig. 5). At this point, the pictorial structure of the painting is almost abstract. A background painted beforehand in relatively plain colors serves as a base onto which successive layers of merged colors can be added.

After these first stages where the paint has been diluted with thinners, start painting more densely colored layers. Touch up the mountains in the background with a little Prussian blue, making sure that their outlines contrast enough with the blue of the sky. The outlines must be clear so that they are not confused with the vegetation. With more neutral colors, and in particular ochre, work on the mountainsides by adding new layers of vegetation (fig. 6).

The object of this exercise is not to make too detailed a reproduction of the landscape, so the roof can be painted with a layer of plain red and the walls of the houses are lighter to highlight them more clearly against the green-ochre landscape in the background. We can make out a few details, such as the windows, doors and chimneys.

4

5

6

Fig. 4. Keep elaborating the middle ground with an irregular range of colors that increase the textured effect of the dense foliage on the mountainsides.

Fig. 5. As you can see, the artist's method involves coloring basic areas and then building them up with shorter strokes.

Fig. 6. Notice how the paint is spread softly over the surface to create the effect of lightness in the vegetation on the hillsides.

7

Trying to detail the houses any more would be an error, because the textured background that we are working on does not allow for too much elegance (fig. 7). Now, we work a little more on the rocks in the foreground, which give a greater sense of depth to the landscape, and darken the vegetation in the middle ground even more, so that they contrast better with the more distant planes. This somewhat blurred and imprecise treatment of the different areas of color lend a certain sense of movement, light and color to the picture (fig. 8).

At this stage, you should use horsehair bristles, be they flat or rounded. The color has thickened as the piece has progressed, even becoming a paste at this final stage (fig. 9).

Although there is not much detail or accuracy, the painting portrays the scene's strength of character. If you try to make the vegetation or the buildings more detailed, you will not find it an easy task because marble powder is a rough, coarse material that does not lend itself very well to meticulous work. You should use a lot of modeling and merging for this painting. The paint is usually applied with the light, rubbing movements of a hard brush. When working on a marble powder background,

8

9

TIPS

–When working on a surface textured with marble powder, you need brushes with resistant bristles, such as horsehair. If you use softer bristles, you will be dismayed at how quickly they get worn. This is because the grainy surface of marble powder is highly erosive when it is rubbed upon.

–If you want to modify the initial texture, try to do it while the paste is still wet. Once it is dry, the paste gets hard, and your only option is to paste another layer on top.

Fig. 7. Detail needs to be minimal, because a textured background is not suitable for highly elaborate work.

Fig. 8. The set of houses has been painted geometrically to contrast with an imprecise background in which colors are superimposed over others with little apparent meaning.

Fig. 9. If we darken the vegetation in the middle ground and add detail to the rocks in the foreground, the composition looks deeper.

10

bear in mind that the texture of the paste will help you to neutralize the color (fig. 10).

You will have almost certainly wondered how you are supposed to go about correcting a mistake when painting on a surface like this. You obviously cannot take the color off with a spatula and paint over it again, as you would do if you were working on a flat surface,

but there is a solution. You should get a cloth (blotting paper is no good because it would tear) and dampen it with a little thinners. Rub it over the area in question and try to get rid of any unwanted paint. Keep rubbing with the cloth until you get the gray color of the marble powder back. Now you can repaint the section.

Fig. 10. Despite the difficulties of working on a marble paste background, the paint in its final state has a remarkable textural and chromatic richness. The combination of oil paints and marble powder is one of the most popular mixed techniques in art today.

Painting Roofs with the *Anticerne* Effect

Now we are going to do a more creative exercise, in which contrasts of color play a fundamental role. We are going to be painting the rooftops of a pretty seaside town using the *anticerne* effect. This is an alternative technique that uses colored backgrounds so that colored strokes appear isolated and surrounded by the color of the background. For this exercise, we are going to be working with the renowned artist Óscar Sanchís.

First, let's look at the model. It is a view of several rows of picturesque rooftops in the Croatian town of Rovinj (fig. 0). The painting is going to use a daring range of colors that play on the contrast between warm colors lit by a bright sun and the cool colors of the buildings in the shadows, shaded by brushstrokes that represent the warm reflections.

We start by covering the background with a light orange color (fig. 1). On colored backgrounds, the image has more body and volume than when it appears on white, even at the preparatory stage. These backgrounds serve to provide a global hue for the superimposed colors and lays out a semi-light color base over which both dark and light colors can be painted. The background color that you are going to paint on needs to be completely dry before you spread any more paint over it,

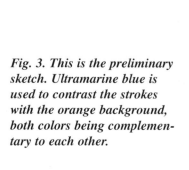

so it might be a good idea to leave the canvas to dry for a few days before you start work. If you like, you can paint the background with acrylic paints because they only take about half an hour to dry. With a small brush loaded with an intense blue, start working on the outline sketch. As you can see, this is a linear drawing, without any coloring in or degradations (fig. 2) (Óscar Sanchís often likes to paint directly, without bothering with any preparatory work, but this time it seems like he has preferred to lay out a few basic outlines). For the preparatory sketch, the artist has used blue because it is orange's complementary color, in other words, the one that will contrast most on an orange background (fig. 3). Start painting the vegetation with dense, opaque colors, using a medium, flat brush. Just a few directional lines, with the bristles well loaded with color, should be enough (fig. 4). Tonal backgrounds like this require opaque painting methods. Veiling is no good here, because white cannot be reflected.

Fig. 3. This is the preliminary sketch. Ultramarine blue is used to contrast the strokes with the orange background, both colors being complementary to each other.

Fig. 0. The model is this pretty aerial view of rooftops in the tourist resort of Rovinj, on the Croatian coast.

Fig. 1. Painters who are used to painting on white are always surprised by the excellent chromatic possibilities of painting over a differently colored background.

Fig. 2. The artist gets straight down to work on the outline sketch, establishing the positions of each of the main compositional elements.

72

Now paint the facades of the nearest houses by combining flesh colors such as pink, ochre, and heavily whitened yellows (fig. 5). Apply small but thick touches of paint, hardly mixing or manipulating them in any way and make sure that each line is established from the very start. On an opaque background like this, the painter bases his work around the creation of lighter tones on the opacity of superimposed pigments.

The darkest and lightest colors are the first to be completed, because the artist's method involves working on the most contrasted colors first and then concentrating on the more subtle, intermediate tones.

As you can see, the different colors are applied with very little mixing at all, in pure primary and secondary tones, producing a bright, shiny and fresh quality. In this way, paint the roof in the foreground with burnt sienna, yellows and reds; the illuminated facades of the buildings with flesh colors; and the shadowed areas with different blues and burnt sienna (fig. 6). With the painting at this stage, notice how the artist does not cover the lines of the preparatory sketch completely. These lines are integrated into the brushstrokes as a central element of the painting (fig. 7). The fluidity, dexterity and vigor of each stroke put a special feeling of freshness into the piece. There is no reason why one cannot combine the sinuousness of soft, wet lines with dry touches of thick paint. At this point, with the base of the painting already firmly established, there is an important and clearly visible interaction between the outline sketch, the brushstrokes and the textures of the roofs.

4

5

6

7

Fig. 7. Colors are mixed simultaneously on the artist's palette and on the surface of the painting to create a wide range of different tones. Look closely at the roofs in the center of the painting.

Fig. 4. We start working on the masses of dark color with a medium brush. The colors are completely opaque, although gaps are left where the background color shows through.

Fig. 5. The first lines are direct and abrupt, using as much paint as our brush can hold.

Fig. 6. We move to the foreground, always important in both natural and urban landscapes, because it needs to guide the artist's eyes towards the center of the piece and raise an interest in the colors.

8

Fig. 9. Colors mixed so freely on the support suggest the different brushmarks and make the painting look far more interesting.

9

Fig. 8. Spontaneity and dexterity with the brush are the keys to compositions like this. You need to forget about the real colors of each item and let your imagination come up with new interpretations.

10

11

Fig. 10. This illustration shows how expressive strokes can be when both thick and opaque oils are combined.

Fig. 11. The subject has been painted in a daring range that plays on the contrast between brightly sunlit warm colors and the cool appearance of the walls in the shadows.

The superimposition of the strokes is tremendous, and the colors appear to be mixed (fig. 8). However, even more definition is needed in the middle and background. Notice how the background color modifies the temperature and atmosphere of the painting, and if you look closely, you will see how the artist has freely mixed two or more colors with the tip of his brush, making each stroke look extremely vivid. The grooved colors reproduce the bristle marks (fig. 10).

With cobalt blue and titanium white, the artist paints the small area of sea with flowing, overlapping strokes that cover (though not in a uniform way) the top section of the painting.

When confronting a painting like this, you need to synthesize the rhythm of the composition by using color, movement and brushstrokes. Notice how the background color appears between the areas of color, provoking contrasts of tone and color. The greatest contrast is between saturated complementary colors. To work with contrast, you need to understand and apply the laws and characteristics of complementary colors (fig. 11).

In the finished painting, you can easily see how, using the anticerne effect, the color and tone of a background influence the appearance of a painting. The background color forms an integral part of the piece as a transition

TIPS

—In general, a coolly colored background, be it green or blue, produces a coldness in the picture, while yellow, red and orange create a sense of warmth.

—The transparency of oil colors increases with time. This is why you should apply thick, opaque colors wherever you need the background to be covered.

—As we are working with intense colors, it is important to wash each brush after each operation, or we will risk dirtying the paint on the canvas.

12

Fig. 12. The finished piece is full of vivid, expressive lines. It has all the immediacy of an alla prima painting, but every aspect has, in fact, been carefully elaborated.

between the different areas of color and to provide glimpses of a neutral shade where the opaque one is just a dry stroke or a very soft veil. The painting may look aggressive at first sight because of the use of so many pure and complementary colors. If you have been practicing alongside the artist, you may have found it difficult to decide how to reorganize the color and forms of the model in your picture, particularly because we have done away with the more tonal effects of local colors. Therefore, you need to avoid degrading colors, mixing or using your fingers to merge thick colors and produce different areas of paint. Your colors must be applied opaquely, as pastes and with the limits of each area of color clearly defined. It is a question of developing your sense of the abstract, which involves selecting the colors and elements of the visual world to create a certain effect, without worrying about representation in the normal sense of the word. What you can never forget when painting with the anticerne method is that, when surrounded by orange, each color is visible in all of its purity and brightness. If you want, try painting the same picture with a white background, and you will see how different the result is. When placed next to orange, colors shine. Next to white, they have deeper tones.

Painting a Garden with Spatulas

Paint applied with a brush can be diluted, concentrated or of medium consistency, but when it is applied with a spatula it always has to be thick to form crests and gaps onto which light and shadow can play. In the next exercise, we shall be finding out how to paint with this strange instrument, and to do so, we shall be working with the sculptor and painter Carlant. Feel free to use guide sheet number four and follow each of the following steps carefully.

We are going to paint the garden of a pretty cottage in Winchester, a town on the outskirts of London. We are not only interested in the texture of the vegetation, but also in the strong contrast between light and shadow (fig. 0).

Before starting, do as the artist does, and draw a simple sketch that outlines the fit and composition. When you are going to use opaque techniques and less delicate treatments, it is best to sketch with charcoal. When you have covered the whole support with thick paint, there is no danger of any of the lines showing through the paint (fig. 1).

On the palette, we start mixing a little ultramarine blue with carmine and plenty of white. This mixture, made in unequal proportions, will be used for the sky, and will have a certain violet appearance. With green and a touch of indigo, roughly color the vegetation in the foreground, worrying more about the color than the form of the undergrowth (fig. 2).

For the vibrant colors of the sky, make short spatula strokes as if you were using a trowel, and to create the clouds, you need to make a rough texture where the colors mix. Do this by moving the tip of the blade energetically, and be generous with the paint, applying enough to fill in the texture of the canvas (fig. 3). At this early stage, it is important to cover all of the white of the paper to avoid simultaneous contrast. White in the background makes it harder to appreciate the colors within the context of the piece, so you need to eliminate it as soon as possible. The first colors need to be wide and generous, with short, irregular strokes that can be applied with a pear-shaped spatula. This way, three or four different tones can

0

1

2

Fig. 0. The artist has chosen this scene of a house and garden on the outskirts of London.

Fig. 1. All oil paintings that use an opaque technique need a preparatory sketch to situate the composition and fit.

Fig. 2. First, you have to color the sky and the vegetation in the foreground, without worrying too much about details.

Fig. 3. Painting with a spatula can, in principle, be more complicated than using a brush, so you will need a lot of practice before you feel comfortable.

3

4

already be seen in the green of the garden, and they will soon start configuring the patterns of light and shadow (fig. 4).

Hold the spatula at different angles, vary the pressure you apply and use different parts of it to produce different lines and effects. The pastes should follow the directions of the blades from the very start, in other words, the textures and forms of the elements. Therefore, the walls of the house will need to be flatter and the profiles much less irregular than those of the trees and plants in the garden (fig. 5).

The shadowed parts of the building have been painted with a mixture of dark grays and gray-violets. The green blanket that covers the garden is also nearing completion. In a painting like this, painted entirely with a spatula, the flat and rough parts of the grass in the garden reflect light in different ways and create an interesting and highly complex surface (fig. 6). Bearing this in mind, study the

5

Fig. 4. Look at the differences in the way the sky (smoother and less degradations) and the vegetation in the foreground (rougher, pastier and less precise) have been treated.

Fig. 5. Start with a thin background and gradually move on to applying thicker layers.

Fig. 6. The directions of the strokes vary, as does the amount of paint applied.

leaves of the tree on the left, in which violet shades can be seen in the shadowed areas, along with cinnabar green, cadmium green and permanent green mixed with ochre and other dark gray colors.

The roof of the house is painted with a touch of ochre and English red; the sunny facades with ochre, sienna and a little white; and the doors and windows with small pastes of mixed colors. For the more subtle effects in the forms of the windows and doors of the house, hold the spatula as you would hold a bow to a violin, supporting the plastic part of the blade with your index finger and pressing the tip onto the surface of the painting, thus applying the paint more meticulously.

Look at the color of the walls of the house, more uniform compared to the rest of the more freely and vigorously painted garden (fig. 7). When you paint the vegetation, you do not only have to use the flat part of the spatula; you can also create sharp, accurate lines with the edge.

6

Now try to expose the more brightly-lit sections of the foreground. To do this, spread thick, ochre, compound green and emerald green pastes mixed with a little white. Similarly, put more shape into the shadows with the use of violets, blue-grays and English red. Spatulas are useful for applying color to the wet surface of the garden without dirtying the color beneath. To do this, load the blade with color and press

few strokes and then adds the few touches of detail that he feels are necessary for the painting to be comprehensible. The overall balance between synthesis and shade that the artist puts into his painting generally boils down to the artist's own personal feelings. Be clear about what you are aiming for before you start painting, and always work with these intentions in mind (fig. 9).

You may have made the mistake of trying to add an oily medium to the paint. As in any pasting method, you should never mix the paint with a diluting agent or medium. If you do, you run the risk of losing the right consistency to conserve the spatula marks. Just as color loses its intensity when it is over-mixed on the palette, directly applied paint loses its freshness if it is rubbed too much against the canvas or

7

Fig. 7. The voluminous pastes used for the vegetation in the foreground add depth to the piece.

lightly on the spatula as you work. The artist makes the tip scrape the paint, thus combining spatula painting with a kind of graffito technique.

Finish off by covering the white of the support and defining the forms better, although you do not need to aim for too much realism. Spatula work does not lend itself very well to highly detailed painting.

The artist keeps moving in just two directions: aiming for synthesis and shade, and alternating between the two. In other words, he paints the most essential of what he sees with just a

8

Fig. 8. The wavy forms, with their energetic textures, were made with the spatula held flatly, while the straight lines were made with its point.

9

if it is applied thoughtlessly. So, don't move the spatula back and forwards. Hold it steadily against the canvas and spread the paint in a single, deliberate movement, lifting the spatula cleanly when the line is finished. There is a danger that each new paste mixes with the one before, which can dirty the colors and blur shapes. Don't be fooled into thinking that paintings made with pastes are more suited to improvisation and free, uninhibited styles. This is anything but the case, and they actually need to be planned very carefully.

Fig. 9. Paintings made with a spatula tend to look irregular and pasty, and because of the flat edges that most blades have, their strokes present a certain geometric distribution.

Painting with the Wet White Technique

The method of painting with the wet white technique is based on the juxtaposition of small touches of relatively pure colors on a surface prepared with a thick coat of white paint, while it is still wet. This experimental technique results in an effective, vibrant painting. For this exercise, we are going to be working in collaboration with the painter and etcher Ester Llaudet.

We are going to use a small, wooden board, primed with latex and whiting. To do this exercise with us, you will need a board that is about a foot long. You can see the chosen model in figure 0. It is a view in the mountainous region in the Northeast of Cuba, near Santiago.

Before starting, the artist spreads a thick coat of lead white mixed with varnish resin over the surface of the support (fig. 1).

There is no preparatory sketch; the painting must be started immediately, while the white paint is still damp. Try to apply the paint in small strokes, modifying the color and tones by controlling and altering the mixture and density of your strokes. Doing this, start by applying ultramarine blue, emerald green, cadmium red and ochre to the bottom, right section of the painting (fig. 2). Keep your colors as pure and clean as you can and distinguish each stroke clearly and gently mix them into the white background.

Keep working on the landscape and draw the outline of the vegetation in the foreground with emerald green. Use ochre, orange and permanent green to complete the middle ground. Finally, use gray, burnt umber and a

Fig. 0. We are going to paint this view of steep mountains in the center of Cuba.

Fig. 1. The first thing you need to do is cover the painting surface with a thick layer of lead white mixed with varnish resin.

Fig. 2. Load a brush with paint (not too liquid) and apply it to the surface in short strokes.

3

little emerald green and ultramarine blue to insinuate the outline of the mountains in the distance (fig. 3). For these first applications of color, the contrast of complementary colors has been exploited, such as that between red and green in the foreground. For the lighter areas, the strokes contain less paint and have been mixed more heavily into the background white. They are based more on the background white than intense colors owing to the transparency of the pigments.

At this stage, there is a clearly neutral effect to the colors in general, produced by a series of superimposed colors that only partially cover the color below (in this case white). This is an optic combination of colors. The opacity of the color progressively darkens the overall tone, but thanks to the spaces between the strokes that the background white can be seen through, the surface stays bright (fig. 4).

Fig. 3. Let the colors mix on the canvas and not the palette.

4

Keep working until all of the initial values of the landscape are finished. Superimpose new strokes, but use more intense colors for the mountains in the distance, to put more detail into this morphology that is so typical of central Cuba. Look closely at how the artist has used shadows with quite unnatural colors like green, blue and turquoise, and has superimposed the grayish tones in the background. With a slightly smaller brush and a touch of burnt umber, the artist has darkened the vegetation in the middle ground. This takes a lot of the flatness out of the image, and gradually produces depth and relief (fig. 5). The stokes may look small and insignificant, but it is impossible to apply a touch of color without it affecting the painting as a whole. For the areas of sky, apply a few light tones of ultramarine blue, letting the white coat beneath show through in the lightest areas. Keep adding new contrasts to the interme-

Fig. 4. Notice how the colors get paler as they move into the distance.

5

Fig. 5. In theory, you should only use primary colors, because these can be mixed to produce secondary and tertiary colors.

diate zone and intensify the colors of the fields with a little yellow ochre (fig. 6).

Now go back to the vegetation in the foreground and superimpose new, irregularly distributed layers of yellow ochre, violet, ultramarine blue and emerald green. A more intense, contrasted foreground creates a more believable sense of space and perspective (fig. 7).

When the colors are seen from a distance, they mix optically to create subtle tonal and color gradations that serve to define the image. In the darker sections, such as the foreground, colors have been used in all their intensity.

To finish the painting, we complete a few details painting the vibrant color of the flowers in the foreground with cadmium red and lemon yellow. The branches of the tree that emerges in the middle of the painting are painted with burnt umber (fig. 8).

As you can see, the finished piece certainly shares many of the characteristics of pointillism. The white coat of paint that we have been painting over increases the effect of the lines and creates a freer, thicker style of painting that is dominated by more pastel-like chromatic ranges (fig. 9). The impact of this delightful painting owes itself, in part, to the mass of bright color. The colors have been carefully chosen to get the right general harmony and, at the same time, the odd touch of contrast. Ultramarine blue and violet have been stretched from the back-

6

7

8

TIPS

—When painting, always be selective. You sometimes need to exaggerate or reduce colors, contrasts and forms in order to balance the harmony of the piece.

—The paint will take a few days to dry, so you have plenty of time for modifications.

Fig. 6. Notice that, to add depth to the piece, small strokes of complementary colors have been added to the previous green.

Fig. 7. We intensify the foreground to give the piece a greater sense of depth.

Fig. 8. Although the idea is not to represent the trees particularly accurately, they are totally convincing.

9

ground to the foreground to unite the composition.

Don't try complicated superimpositions of colors, and don't use too much paint at once, or the painting will look too pasty. Use separate brushstrokes and don't work too much on any one spot, or you will either take off the white from below or create a confused mess. To avoid errors, always have a piece of wood that is also covered in lead white handy. You will find it useful for testing out effects before using them on the painting itself.

Fig. 9. The white wet technique is a characteristic example of how to apply small touches of color to elaborate a painting. Seen from afar, the intense chromatic effects create a vividly shiny landscape.

Urban Landscape with Fusion Techniques

Markets, cafes and streets are interesting subjects to paint, because they offer us a wide range of effects, textures and forms. And that is exactly what Carlant is going to do in this exercise, paint a street with pedestrians using fusion techniques. Although one of the main effects of oil paintings is the use of heavy brushstrokes, another of its most characteristic aspects is that brush marks can be hidden by mixing and softening. I suggest that you do this exercise with the artist on guide sheet number five.

For this step by step exercise, the subject is going to be a street in the old quarter of Bern, Switzerland (fig. 0). As you can see, the subject offers a powerful sense of space, not only derived from the point of view or the typical style of houses, but also the rainy weather, which appears in the image in the form of grays, ochres and violets that contrast with the warmer appearance of the sky.

Let's start. For painting with such a strong tonal structure, a sketch with dark, gray colors can be very effective. Do as the artist does and start off with a brush drawing (fig. 1).

Fig. 0. Carlant is going to paint this picture of a wide street in the old town quarter of Bern in Switzerland.

Fig. 1. If you plan to paint a picture with a lot of merging and blending, it is a good idea to make a sketch with the lines drawn with a brush.

Pre-paint with gray, opaque tones, which will give you the chance to concentrate on the forms and tonal values of the subject before having to make any decisions with regard to color. Work on the sky in the same way. Use two degraded colors for this - Naples yellow and a little carmine. The presence of carmine should be more evident as you approach the horizon (fig. 2). With somewhat more intense colors, sketch the figure with his back turned and the fountain in the foreground.

At this early stage, the artist is using just as much diluted paint as thick paint, and sometimes mer-

Fig. 2. The subject is constructed with light grays over which thicker colors are superimposed. A mixture of carmine and Naples yellow is used for the sky.

ges very diluted colors over thicker layers. With a small brush and a touch of ochre and raw umber, he has sketched the sculpted figure that appears on the left-hand facade. In a similar way, he has added this color to other parts of the painting, such as the hair of the person with his back turned and one of the cars on the right (fig. 3).

Fig. 3. After a short while, the white of the paper is covered with the first values of rather dull colors.

As you can see, the artist constructs the forms by merging the colors with the layers below. Merging, softening and blending techniques make the surface look smoother and rid the picture of the presence and immediacy of straight lines, replacing them with a softer, more global treatment (fig. 4). You should do the same.

The arches and windows of the facades have been painted using merging, brushing thin layers of opaque paint over another color that remains visible in places and plays an important role in the appearance of the painting. The limits between one color and another are not so clear, they are rather imprecise and blurred (fig. 5).

The figures have been painted with the minimum of detail but the results are convincing enough because of the care that has gone into their postures, clothes and movements (fig. 6). To get these results, work with a small brush.

If you paint the picture in just one session, you will find it easier to get the progressive graduations of color and tone right. This is because the painting stays damp long enough for a larger series of colors and tones to be spread. You will see that the windows in the facades are less detailed and more blurred the further away they are. To do this, use a fanned brush like a feather duster to flatten or blend the colors.

4

5

6

Fig. 4. The depth of color in the facades of the streets has been created with a series of superimposed, merged colors that produce subtle degradations.

Fig. 5. The way of harmonizing the different areas of gray and violet colors is the unifying factor of space in the painting.

Fig. 6. This illustration shows how the outlines of the groups of people have been blended into the surrounding tones. Different brushes have been used for the task.

Used like this, the brush merges the colors together but keeps them separate (fig. 7).

Once the effect of depth, or perspective, has been established, paint the details of the fountain in the foreground. Use more intense colors that will show up against the other tones in the picture. If necessary, you now have to create more contrasts so that the painting looks more three-dimensional.

This is when we stop to analyze the development of the painting. You can see how the artist has used low key colors, to create a rather dull, but more delicate and subtle, chromatic tendency. The colors are not saturated, but neutral and reduced (fig. 8).

And here is the finished painting (fig. 9). You may have had problems constructing the depth of the image. For a subject like this, you need to think carefully about the perspective of the buildings. It is not difficult if we remember the basic rule that the parallel lines will always join on the horizon. If the perspective is wrong, a building or view of a street can look rather unconvincing. Proportion is just as important. The windows in the facades, the sizes of the people – they all need to look right in relation to each other. The width and height of a

7

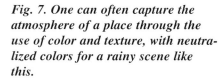

Fig. 7. One can often capture the atmosphere of a place through the use of color and texture, with neutralized colors for a rainy scene like this.

Fig. 8. The overall neutrality gives an extraordinary force to the dull colors of an overcast day.

8

TIPS

–Normally, paintings like this are based on sketches or the combination of studies and photographs because people are never going to stay in the same place long enough for you to paint them from nature.

–All city streets have a characteristic atmosphere. So, when you decide to paint an urban landscape, try to recapture that atmosphere and find the essential elements that portray the character and feeling of the place.

–If you want to soften your tones even more, you can use a sable brush on the surface of the painting, following along the borders of different colors.

9

building must relate to each other properly, and check the sizes of the doors and arches. The painting may look too floury, which means there is too much white. You need to realize that adding a color does not have to mean adding white too. Colors can also be lightened with (among others) Naples yellow, ochre, cadmium yellow or sky blue. If you have been merging, the result may look too uniform, with too few contrasts and therefore, too little relief. After softening, the most normal thing to do is to mark the darker and lighter tones and repaint them during the final stage.

Fig. 9. Inexpert painters try to avoid urban landscapes, but the exercise on these pages shows just how stimulating the many possibilities of this subject can be.

Painting a Group of Musicians

In this exercise you can put everything that you have learned so far into practice as we take on a new theme, that of the human figure. The painting shows a group of moving people. If you want to produce paintings like this, you will find that this is a good place to start, with people who do not vary their posture very much. The painting is going to combine opaque techniques with veils. Once again, we are honored by the presence of the artist Josep Antoni Domingo. If you want to try the same task, you can do it on guide sheet number six.

As always, the artist first spends a few minutes observing his subject and thinking about which details he is going to concentrate on in particular. With a number 2 pencil, synthesize the general appearance of the group with just a few lines. As you observe and draw, keep each person's pose fixed in your mind. Notice how, although it is a synthetic drawing, the artist has found the proportions between the different figures and has applied a light shadow so that the patterns of light are clear from the very start. See how, with just a few lines, he has already suggested the texture of their clothes (fig. 1).

When you have accurately drawn the sketch, you can start painting. Like the artist, you should start by coloring the figure to the right. From the start, try to recreate the volume of the figures and reflect the areas of more or less light, superimposing layers of color. To get the right tone for painting skin, mix titanium white with ochre yellow and vermilion. With a thin brush, add more vermilion to the pinkest areas, and a touch of cobalt blue to the darker areas under the first person's chin. The same blue, mixed with burnt umber, is what you need to recreate the color and texture of the folds in his trousers. For his shirt, the artist has settled for using the white of the canvas. With a few simple, gray lines, he has

Fig. 0. This time we are going to paint this lively group of Irish musicians.

Fig. 1. Whenever we paint figures and portraits, we need a preparatory drawing. If not, you could easily make structural errors.

Fig. 2. The artist starts with the most general features, but treats each figure as a different portrait.

Fig. 3. As you can see, the background and figures are developed at the same time so as to create a sense of atmosphere.

88

defined the creases along his arm. A simple vermilion color should be enough for the second person's jersey. For his hair, the artist has used burnt umber, adding yellow to indicate the lighter parts. For the guitar, he has used light ochre with a touch of white, to which he has added burnt umber for the darker tones of the fretboard. As this is not a static, studio pose, the artist has used a background made up of impressionistic brushstrokes that seem to generate more atmosphere. At the top, he has made a degradation out of cobalt blue, yellow and white mixed with burnt umber and gray-green, and, at the bottom, cobalt blue (fig. 2).

As you can see, the artist has borne several things in mind up until this stage. The proximity between the real life colors and the ones that he has chosen has been achieved through synthetic applications of color and simultaneously dealing with the figures and the background.

Once you have started defining the colors of one figure, start thinking about the next. Just like in the previous phase, start by applying layers of color and then use a thinner brush to add specific details (fig. 3). The brownish mixtures that you made before can also be used for the jacket and hair. Notice how the artist, through the direction of his brushstrokes, recreates the textures and folds in the clothes and applies touches of light and shadow here and there as he searches for details in the foreground. Use the white of the canvas once again for the trousers, and shadow them with gray touches. Do

4

5

6

Fig. 4. The painting advances meticulously from left to right, gradually revealing the forms and postures of the people in the picture.

Fig. 5. The figures in the foreground need to be more detailed and better defined than those sitting further away.

Fig. 6. The picture is more colorful now, and we move on to the textures of the clothes and making each person look lifelike.

the same as the artist, and keep working on the background, adding a little yellow to the mixture as you add more detail to the figure at the back.

Keep on working, applying new values to the figures in the background and take advantage of the mixtures of color that you already have on your palette to paint the others. Volume can be created by representing the textures of skin and clothes (fig. 4). When an artist paints a human figure, he needs to study, within the limits of his chosen palette, the most appropriate range of flesh colors for that particular subject. For this picture, he has mixed different proportions of ochre, red, blue and white.

He works on each figure separately, but adds details to them all at the same time, thus creating a better sense of unity. An exercise like this requires experience and artistic mastery (figs. 5 and 6).

The artist takes a few moments to relax and think about how his painting is developing. You should take several such breaks as you work, as it will take several sessions to be completed.

Now it is time to work on the details that are going to produce the required effect. As the artist gets nearer to completing the painting, the figures have more body and their facial features are more defined. Look how he has reproduced the strings and the opening in the guitar, and try to copy his style (fig. 7).

The artist keeps working on the rest of the piece. He tries to get the right textures and volumes for each item of clothing, making the creases and folds even more detailed. Now, with a thin brush, shade the shadows on the white trousers, making the figure in the foreground more important. Notice how his shoes do not shine as much as his other clothes, which helps to recreate the texture of leather (fig. 8).

Fig. 7. Use a thinner brush for details. This is probably the task that puts your skills most to the test.

Fig. 8. Try to create the different clothing textures by superimposing more intense colors than the real life material.

8

TIPS

–For practice, paint simple sketches from nature, using different layers of color. At first, choose scenes in which the people are not likely to move very much.

–The preparatory sketch of these people should be drawn quickly because you will only have a few seconds to visualize the postures that you are going to draw.

–Don't define the background too much, just suggest imprecise forms with diluted colors instead of solid forms that would take the focus away from the central theme and make your ideas less comprehensible.

9

And the exercise ends here (fig. 9). The artist has achieved a detailist result that, along with a richly shaded background, puts life and expressiveness into the exercise. Surely, when you try a similar exercise from nature, you will find it difficult to make your initial drawing accurate. Try to synthesize forms and pay attention to form rather than detail as you draw. For a general evaluation of contrasts between light and shadow, squint your eyes and you will see how the forms look clearer and darker. The most difficult aspect might be painting the facial features. Remember that in order to paint lifelike representations of human features you do not have to be a great drawer. If this aspect of your work is still not very well developed, leave the face quite blurred and roughly-sketched without paying too much attention to detail. Another difficult factor is the different treatment of the textures and qualities of material, such as the folds in the clothes and the flat surface of some of the instruments. This not such an easy factor to avoid. If it seems complicated, try to practice painting objects wrapped in cloth or paint the folds in the clothing using veils, because that way the margin of error is not so wide. These are usually painted in the same color as the clothes in real life, but somewhat dirtier and more intense than the original color. Use short, deliberate strokes.

In principle, painting figures in movement is a complex process, but with enough practice, your results will certainly improve.

Fig. 9. The painting is finished. It transmits a sensation of action and movement as if time has been frozen for an instant. Don't feel too disappointed if your first attempt is somewhat unsatisfactory.

Portrait of a Young Lady

Ester Llaudet, who has already worked with us on earlier exercises, is now going to paint a young lady's face. This can be one of the most difficult tasks that an amateur artist ever has to face, but it is also one that no self-respecting book on oil painting could ever leave out. The model is this girl's smiling face (fig. 0). As you can see, her head is viewed frontally and her body is facing slightly to the right.

Before you put your brush to paper, study the model carefully. Make a mental note of the facial features, proportions, lights and colors that you see. After a few minutes' observation, you can start. To draw well, not only do you need skill and talent, but you also need to know how to observe.

Before anything, draw the symmetrical axis with charcoal, and then a square frame. Both of these will help to lay out the proportions and angle of her face. Now draw the girl's facial features synthetically, highlighting contrast with your charcoal stick and blurring the areas of shadow (fig. 1).

With the charcoal portrait complete, Ester now finds the colors that she will need for coloring the face. She mixes white, ochre and vermilion for the illuminated parts and burnt umber with a few touches of Prussian blue for the shadowed areas. Then she starts oil painting, superimposing different layers of color as she builds up the face (fig. 2).

Next, work on the eyes and lips by modeling the flesh of her skin with different intensities of flesh colors, making the contrasts of light and shadow more potent, as it is in them that the strength of the girl's expression resides (fig. 3).

Pay a great deal of attention to the lips and eyes, because these two facial elements are fundamental in making your painting look like the person. Once you have painted them, move on to the hair and eyebrows, using burnt umber mixed with ochre yellow and cadmium red to get the mahogany-like effect of the reflections in her hair (fig. 4). Paint her teeth with a watery burnt umber and a thin brush.

Notice how the tonality of the model's face changes. The pink color of her skin becomes less intense when it contrasts with the dark brown of her hair. The tonality of a color will always depend on the colors that surround it.

Take a break, and look at the painting globally, then keep working on the look in the girl's eyes until it is as similar as you can make it to the model's. Apply reflections of light to the pupils and with a mixture of the tone of the skin and burnt umber, define the outline of her eyes and the shadow of her eyelashes with a thin brush (fig. 5).

With the same brush, put more volume into her lips. Apply more intense colors on the right than on the left, where her lips are more brightly-lit. Construct the form of her nose by creating subtle variations of flesh color. To do this, mix unequal proportions of pink with ochre, burnt umber and raw sienna (fig. 6).

Fig. 1. Ester wants to capture the spontaneity of the model's expression, which requires a quick and skillfully drawn sketch.
Fig. 2. Without making the features too precise, Ester looks for a lifelike representation and the right facial proportions.
Fig. 3. The first areas of color establish the areas of light and shadow on the face. This is done by adding a little burnt umber to the original flesh color.
Fig. 4. Once the general picture is complete, concentrate on the lips and eyes, possibly the two most important aspects of the face.

5

Fig. 5. At this stage, the painting is starting look very similar to the model.

Fig. 6. The eyes are outlined with a thin brush, the nose is constructed and the lips are formed.

Fig. 7. Work the background with an ultramarine blue and titanium white background.

When you have finished painting the basic features of her face, try to make it more expressive by accentuating contrasts between light and shadow and defining volume.

Once this stage is over, Ester applies a degradation to the background, mixing ultramarine blue with white, highlighting the front of the figure. Use the same base color that you used on her face to color her cleavage (fig. 7). Follow these same steps and spend a little time getting the color of this part of her body right, along with her dress and a few final touches to the background. Before considering your painting complete, you should work a little more on the color of her flesh. Think about contrasts, degradations, anatomy and shadows (fig. 8). As you will have seen from the portrait, the model has been represented within a warm color range. This way, the artist transmits the warm-hearted nature of the girl, and intensifies the rosy color of her skin and the mahogany-like reflections in her hair.

There is a good chance that, when you do a similar exercise, you forget that if you want coherent results, you need to develop the painting as a whole as you go along. If you do not do this, it will not be harmonized enough to look like the model.

6

7

8

Fig. 8. The finished piece is a valuable study of the female face, painted by the artist in less than a day.

93

Glossary

A

Agglutinate. Substance that is mixed with powdered pigment to make a medium of painting.

Alla prima. Direct painting technique that involves painting quickly in just one session and never going back over what one has painted.

B

Blending. Procedure that involves softening contours and areas of contact between colors to form gentle gradations.

C

Chiaroscuro. Rembrandt was a master of chiaroscuro. In his work, forms and colors are clearly visible despite being surrounded by intense shadows. In his books on painting, Parramón defines chiaroscuro as "the art of painting light over shadow".

Chromatic harmony. The balanced relationship of different colors within a painting.

Composition. The balanced and harmonized distribution of the different elements that appear in a picture. Composing involves bearing these factors in mind as one selects the best arrangements.

Covering capacity. The capacity that a color has to dominate other colors in mixtures and veils.

D

Degradation. Reducing the value of a tone, gradually making it more intense or softer, so that the transition is gradual rather than abrupt.

Dry brush. Painting technique that involves applying thick paint to the support, so that it sticks to both the pores in the canvas and the texture of the paint on the surface.

F

Film. Layer of paint or coating over the surface.

Fit. Preliminary drawing that establishes the basic structure of bodies as simple geometric forms (cubes, rectangles, prisms etc) that are often known as frames.

G

Genre. Classification of artistic techniques, such as still lives, landscapes, figures and interiors.

I

Induction of complementaries. A phenomenon derived from simultaneous contrasts, which complies with the norm that states that "to modify a particular color, you simply need to change the color that surrounds it".

L

Local color. The genuine color of an object when it is not affected by shadow, reflections or other factors.

M

Medium. Liquid in which pigments are held, for example linseed oil is used for oil paints and acrylic resin for acrylics. Pastel sticks can be mixed or dampened in any of these mediums.

Merging. Technique that involves spreading or reducing one or more layers of color onto to a background layer, so that the lower layer is still visible through the superimposed one.

Mixed techniques. Using different painting procedures in the same picture, or using a combination of different supports.

Modeling. Although this is a sculptural term, it can also be applied to painting and drawing to refer to the way in which different tones are applied to create an illusion of the third dimension.

O

Opacity. The capacity that a gray shade or wash has for covering a layer below it. Opacity varies from pigment to pigment.

Opaque painting technique. Pastel technique that involves applying thick layers of color to create a textured surface with little or no merging.

P

Pasting. Technique that involves applying thick layers of color to create textured surfaces.

Perspective. Way of representing the three-dimensional world on a two-dimensional surface.

Pigments. Coloring agents in powdered form that are obtained from natural sources (although some are now made synthetically) that, when mixed with an agglutinate, create paint.

Pointillism. Painting technique that involves applying small dots to the canvas.

Pre-painting. Preliminary paint that the rest of the colors of a piece are painted over.

Preparatory sketch. The preliminary stage in the construction of a drawing or painting, from which the definitive piece can be derived. Several sketches might be made before the artist decides upon the idea he wants to work with.

Primer. Adhesive or gelatinous material that is applied to the canvas before it is painted, making the support less absorbent. It can also be used as an agglutinate in paint.

Proportion. The relationship of one part with the tonality of a piece.

S

Saturation. Value or chromatic degree of a color. Strength of a color that a surface can reflect.

Graffito. Technique that involves scraping a layer of color with a sharp instrument, so that the color of the support becomes visible.

Solvents. Liquids used for dissolving oil paints. The solvent for water based colors is water and for oil based products, turpentine essence, thinners and similar substances are used.

Stanley knife. Sharp knife used for cutting paper, made up of a metal blade inside a plastic handle.

Style. In sculpture, drawing and painting, this is the way that the task is approached. It can be agitated, brusque, delicate, slow, fast... It determines the manner of working of each individual artist.

Support. Surface used for painting or drawing, such a board, sheet of paper or canvas.

T

Texture. Tactile and visual quality of the surface of a drawing or painting. It can be smooth, granulated, rough or cracked.

Tonal background. Opaque coloring in which the color is mixed with white to spread the color in a uniform way. A tonal background can also be colored.

Tonal color. Color offered by the shadow of objects.

Tone. Term that has its origins in music that, when applied to art, refers to the strength and relief of all the parts of a painting with respect to light and color.

Transparency. Way of applying color so that light or the previous layer of color filters through.

V

Value. As much in drawing as painting, volume or modeling is obtained from the tonal values of the model. At the same time, it is achieved through the comparison and tonal resolution of effects of light and shadow.

Veils. Layers of transparent color that are superimposed over the preliminary color when it is dry.

Viscosity. Measure of the characteristic fluidity of a color or medium.

Volatility. Evaporation potential of a solution.

Volume. Three-dimensional effect of a model in the two-dimensional space of a painting.

W

Wet on wet painting. Technique that involves painting over an area of recently applied paint while it is still damp. The level of dampness can be controlled, depending on the effect that the artist wishes to create.

Whiting. Ground, washed chalk that is used for priming cloth and in the composition of pastels.

Acknowledgements

The author would like to thank the following companies and people for their help with the publication of this volume of the *Techniques and exercises* series. Gabriel Martín Roig for his help with the texts and the general coordination of the book; Mónica Mosso for her help with the texts; Antonio Oromí for his photography; Vicenç Piera of the Piera company for his help and advice concerning painting and drawing materials and utensils; Manel Úbeda of Novasis for help with the publication and production of the photography and Photostatting; Olga Bernad, Eva Mª Durán and Ani Amor for granting us permission to use certain photographs as models for painting, and a special thanks to the artists Carlant, Josep Antoni Domingo, Grau Carod, Ester Llaudet, Óscar Sanchís and Teresa Trol.